ARTHUR SWINSON was born in 1 _____ le
attended St Albans School and l_____ et
at Sandhurst Military College, _____ire
Regiment. During the Second World War he served in the infantry and
the Indian army, seeing action in India, Assam, Burma and Malaya.

After the war he joined the BBC to become a senior producer of documentaries. He left the BBC in 1961 to pursue a career as a full time freelance writer, with 300 plays for television, radio and theatre, and over 30 books of fiction and non-fiction to his name. *Writing for Television* is a standard work on the subject. Other works range from *The Great Air Race* to *The Orchid King*, a biography of the leading orchid hunter Frederick Sander. Swinson became a well known military historian, and his book *Kohima*, an account of the battle in which he took part, is widely regarded as one of the best works on the Second World War.

He died in 1970, leaving a widow and three children.

Other works by Arthur Swinson include

Non-Fiction

Wingate in Peace and War (Editor)
Writing for Television
Writing for Television Today
Television in the Making (Conributor)
Television (Junior Reference Library)
Six Minutes to Sunset (Amritsar 1919)
A Casebook of Medical Detection
Kohima
North-West Frontier
The Great Air Race
Four Samurai
The Desert Raiders
The Memoirs of Private Waterfield (Editor, with Donald Scott)
Register of Regiments and Corps of The British Army (Editor)
Frederick Sander: The Orchid King

Fiction
The Temple

Plays

The Bridge of Estaban
Admetus
The Sword is Double-edged
The Senora and other plays

Crime

Sergeant Cork's Casebook
Sergeant Cork's Second Casebook

Adventure
The Siege of Saragoda

Scotch on the Rocks

The True Story Behind Whisky Galore

ARTHUR SWINSON

Luath Press Limited

EDINBURGH

www.luath.co.uk

First published 1963 by Peter Davies, London
This edition 2005

The paper used in this book is recyclable. It is made from
low-chlorine pulps produced in a low-energy, low-emission manner
from renewable forests.

Printed and bound by
Bookmarque Ltd., Croydon

Typeset in 10.5pt Sabon

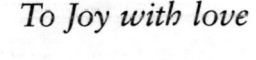

To Joy with love

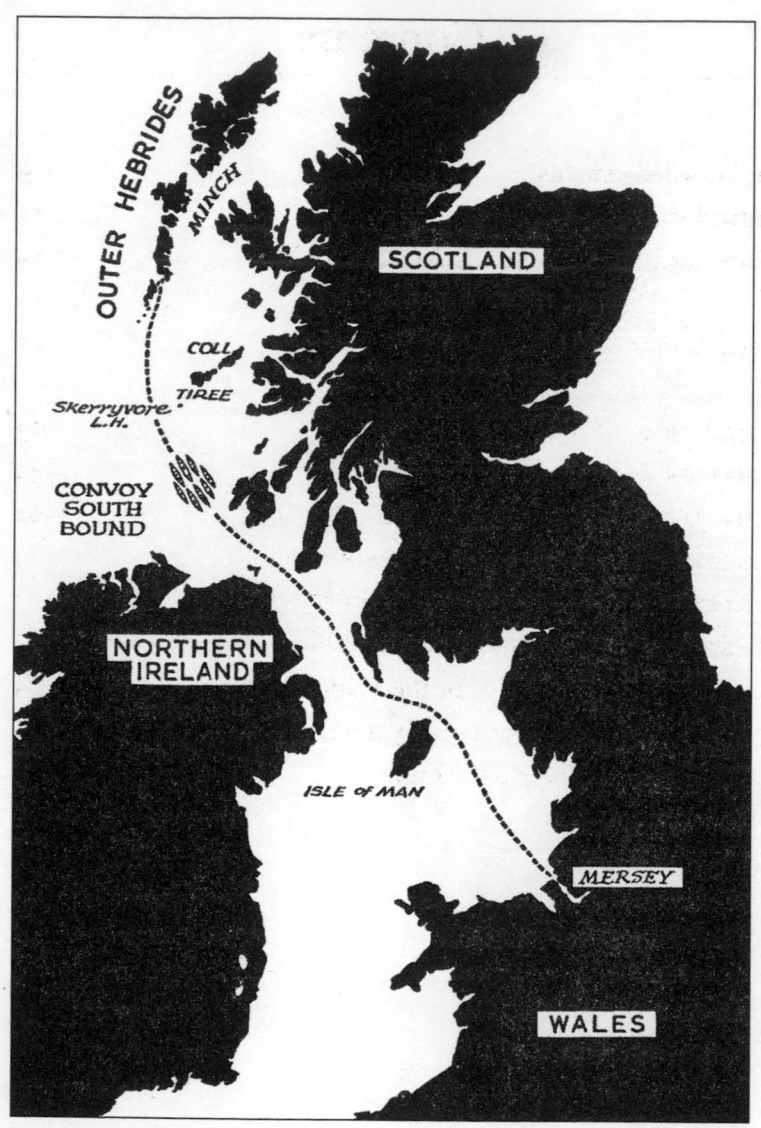

Contents

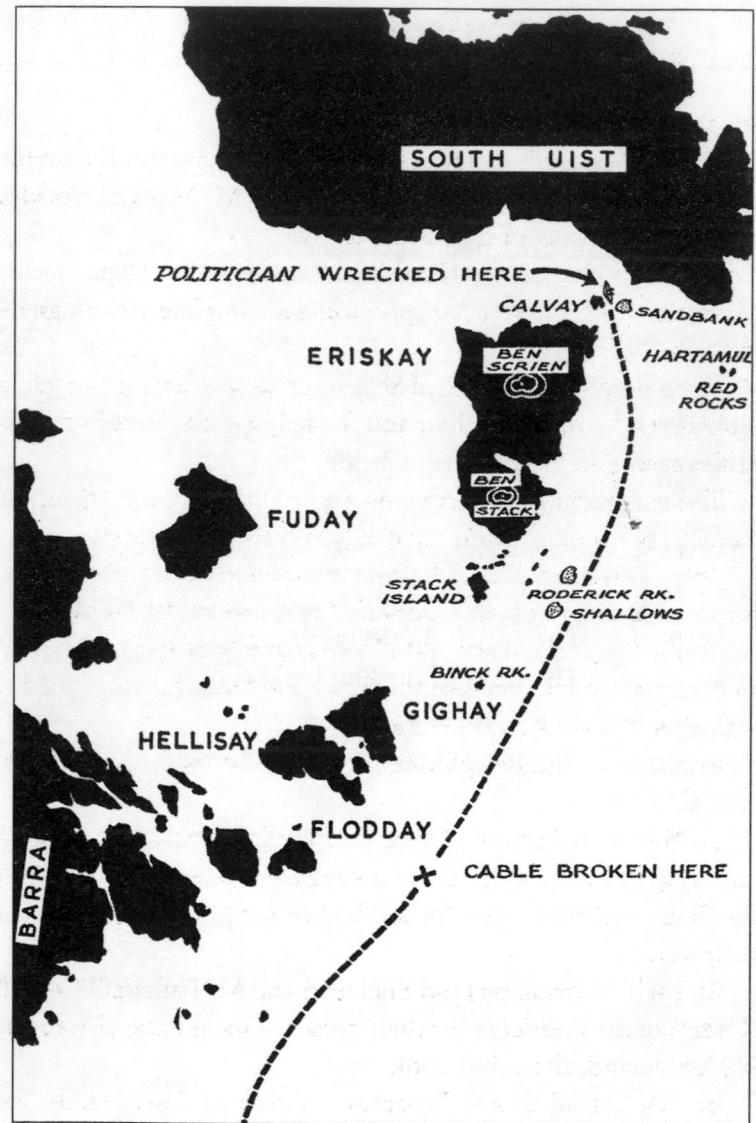

Acknowledgements

MY THANKS ARE DUE

To Her Majesty's Commissioners of Customs and Excise for making available official documents; also to Mr Maurice Nockles and Mr F G Evans of this Department.

To Mr D H Dickens, Head of the Information Department, Messrs Lloyd's, London, for providing a complete set of signals from the *Politician*.

To the Registrar General of Shipping and Seamen for providing a photostat of the ship's log, and for helping me trace members of the crew.

To the Superintendent, Meteorological Office (Edinburgh), Air Ministry, for information regarding weather conditions.

To the Hydrographer, Hydrographic Department, Admiralty, for information regarding tides and currents in the Hebrides.

To the Secretary, the Royal National Lifeboat Institution, and to Mr Allan MacDonald of the Barra Lifeboat, for information regarding the rescue of the crew.

To the GPO (Edinburgh) for providing the map of the undersea cable.

To Dr W Bullerwell (Chief Geophysicist) and Mr T R M Lawrie (District Geologist) for geological information regarding the Outer Hebrides; also for kindly allowing me to quote from their letters.

To Mr T Huntington (2nd Engineer) and Mr Fothergill Cottrell (Cadet) of the *Politician* for their personal memories; also to Mr H I Strickland, the ship's cook.

To Mr David Shaw, Procurator-Fiscal of Lochmaddy for tracing court records.

To Mr Leslie Harrison, General Secretary of the Mercantile

Marine Service Association; and to Mr Owen, head of the Marine Department, for helping me trace officers of the *Politician*.

To the editorial staff of *Sea Breezes* for providing material for the biography of the *Politician*.

To Mr Ivan Gledhill, late Surveyor of HM Customs, for his help and advice.

To Mr P E Holden, late of Messrs Arnott, Young & Co., for material regarding the shipbreaking operations.

To the inhabitants of South Uist who kindly gave me their stories; especially Norman MacMillan, Angus John Campbell, John Curry, and Peter MacInnes. Also to John McIsaac and Donald MacDonald of Eriskay, and Kenneth McCormick, formerly of Barra.

To Colonel Charles Cameron for his help and advice while I was in the Outer Hebrides.

And finally to Sir Compton Mackenzie who first brought the story of the *Politician* to the notice of the world, for his advice, and for generously offering to write the foreword.

Introduction to the 2005 Edition

EARLY IN 2005, with the arrival of the Freedom of Information Act, the SS *Politician* began to resurface with the news that apart from the 250,000 bottles of whisky, there was £3m in currency on board, much in Jamaican 10s. notes. Given that the ship was initially bound for the Caribbean in that cold February in 1941, conspiracy theories swirled: that this was spending money intended for the Windsors, in case Hitler had invaded and they had decided not to wait to look the East End in the face after all; or hush money for the former king and his wife, that Winston Churchill was up to his neck in the *Politician's* preparation. Whatever the truth, these reports fed a growing fascination, with what really happened, already stoked by press reports of a remake of the film of Compton Mackenzie's bestselling novel *Whisky Galore*. It seems this was time to take a new look at this dusty slice of Scottish wartime history, indeed to reclaim it for today's devolved, self-confident Scotland. Yet in all the excitement, it was widely acknowledged that though long out of print, Arthur Swinson's *Scotch on the Rocks*, the original true story of what really happened, has never been surpassed.

In 1962, while researching for a programme series on Customs and Excise my father had the opportunity to spend several weeks on the islands interviewing those who had been part of the story. He had originally heard about the SS *Politician* a few days after it was wrecked, while stationed in northern India. It seems it was the wonder in the face of the Scotsman who told him about it which stuck in his mind. This was magic, a world away from the dusty terrors of warfare. Real drama in an improbable setting. And whisky, thousands of bottles of it. Just lying off shore waiting for rescue . . .

In September 2005, I was asked to write a piece for *The Scotsman* and my family and I travelled in Arthur's footsteps to Lochboisdale in South Uist. As the ferry brought the sharp beauty of the landscape into view, early childhood memories surfaced: my father returning to our home in Hertfordshire after weeks away with an old whisky bottle he said was treasure from a shipwreck, which was filled with the whitest sand I had ever seen. He also brought a blue and yellow tartan blanket which for years served as a tree house tent or a magic carpet for me and my siblings, Sabra and Sheridan. I also have a later memory of arriving at Freshers' Week at Edinburgh University and being surprised when a lecturer told me that almost everyone I would meet in Scotland aged over forty would have a copy of *Scotch on the Rocks* in their bookshelves.

It is the scale of the reality which is striking to any visitor, reared on repeat showings of the 1949 Ealing comedy. The ss *Politician* was no puffer boat, but a 7,900 ton cargo ship, and a key player in the nation's merchant fleet. The channel where it hit the rocks is narrow, the waters shallow enough to have made the ship tower over the landscape and the islanders' small craft with their swinging Tilly lamps. The islanders themselves would have also been not the jolly rogues of Brigadoon caricature, but literate, thinking individuals, part of a cohesive community imbued with highly evolved, business-like values of integrity and self reliance.

In 1941, despite the shortages, they would also have been economically far better off than many of their rationed country-men on the mainland, with plentiful supplies of herring, meat and eggs. Major shipwrecks and the resulting stimulus to the local economy were far from uncommon. As my father recorded, there had been no fewer than eight ships which had run aground in the immediate area, three occurring in quick succession at that time. This was business as usual.

Sir Compton Mackenzie memorably described his bestseller *Whisky Galore* as 'a modern fairy tale'. Few could argue with its enduring magic. Yet on the islands unexpectedly, I encountered strong feelings that his book had actually done them a disservice. That this unlikely founder of the Scottish National Party – in real life an actor's son from West Hartlepool – had concocted a Gaelic speaking paradise of canny peasant crofters to bolster his own successful reinvention as a patrician Scot, fixing the Hebrides for all time in a feudal, tourist time warp.

Perhaps to find the true story, it needed another Englishman, one with no pretensions to any Scots heritage whatsoever, to ask the difficult questions. For the true story, as Arthur Swinson found after weeks researching on the islands, was a grittier, far more textured affair, which curdled into island life with few neat and happy endings. The treatment of those jailed – men supposed to give their lives to defend their country in wartime, remember – was shameful. Neither authorities nor islanders were unscathed by the *Politician*.

As he writes, 'to anyone who insists on a moral, one can only state I think, that faced with these extraordinary circumstances, the rash became rasher, the drunken more drunken, the avaricious more avaricious, the convivial more convivial, the generous more generous, the treacherous more treacherous, the selfish more selfish, and the commercial more commercial.'

These were real flesh and blood people experiencing the full heat of a gold rush: the sudden discovery of free supplies for all, of a valuable, bountiful and highly portable commodity.

It was always a mystery how on earth my father – very much

the moustachioed, Sandhurst and public school educated English army officer – could ever have persuaded the islanders to open up. Yet Arthur was no posturing Captain Waggett, but someone who had grown up through the Depression with few luxuries, winning his way on scholarships with ambitions to be a major playwright, at a time when the theatre so captured the imagination of young men in a hurry.

Arthur was larger than life, loved people and could create a party with his stories. It must also have helped that he was generous to a fault when buying his round! However, I believe it was principally through his seven years in the 'Forgotten Army', serving in Burma, India, Assam and Malaya, that he found the means to connect to Hebrideans, so many of whom had shared his experience.

Scotch on the Rocks is therefore as much a journey of self discovery, as that of the celebrated ship. Page after page, you can feel that south east England stress slipping off Arthur's shoulders, as he encounters the kindliness, prickliness and integrity of island life, and begins to process the trauma of his own war years. Open minded, with a nose for truth and a fine eye for detail, he cuts the islanders some slack, seeing them as neither cut out cardboard thugs or heroes, just people getting on with their lives in a world unfamiliar to him. *Scotch on the Rocks* remains an extraordinary piece of travel writing, vividly evoking a Hebridean way of life which had changed little since wartime.

The manuscript has not been updated or amended apart from the correction of local names which were misspelt in official documents, but deserves to be seen in its own terms, in its own time. Arthur was an Englishman, writing for a predominantly English public. The cultural references are therefore of his time and place, interesting in their own right to a modern audience.

Scotsmen back then were indeed affectionately referred to as Jocks, and as, back in St Albans, Arthur would eat his dinner every night with my mother at 8 pm, he may perhaps be forgiven early on in the book when describing the Scottish high tea taken at 5 pm as an 'abomination'. (Though he redeems himself later by relishing a 'delightful Scottish tea'.) As Moray McLaren writing in *The Scotsman* at the time observed, 'It is most interesting to follow this Englishman's conversion. Is his presentation of his conversion [to the islands' way of life] deliberate art, or is it a result of writing his book as it happened to him? In any event, it is most effective.'

It is also interesting for modern readers to see how attitudes have changed. When Arthur wrote the book, wartime rationing had ended only a few years earlier, and with the 1960s yet to swing into action, deference ruled. Like all his generation who had lived so intensely through World War Two, he retained a faith in national institutions, the landed Establishment and centralised Westminster government, which may strike today's reader as poignant, especially north of the border! But what makes the narrative sparkle is that he did not hesitate to rattle cages and refused to take no for an answer. As we read, we are swept along in his enthusiasm to find out the truth.

Arthur did not have the advantages of the Internet, nor any Freedom of Information Act. In the early '60s wartime 'D' Notices still bristled. Yet how he managed to get round official-dom and solve the mystery of why the *Politician* ran off course remains a masterly piece of detective work. Best of all, Arthur Swinson was a storyteller, with an energetic, sparse prose style which remains refreshingly contemporary. As the London *Evening Standard* observed at the time, *Scotch on the Rocks* is 'vastly entertaining'.

As my father concluded, 'this story happened to the right people and at the right time. In a chaotic world, this does not happen often; and when it does, it should be recorded.'

The true story of the *Politician* remains as fascinating as ever and I am delighted that his masterly work can now be enjoyed by a new generation.

Arthur Swinson died an untimely death from a heart attack aged 54, just seven years after *Scotch on the Rocks* was published. In total, he wrote over 30 books, mainly military history, as well as 300 radio and TV plays and documentaries, and even a musical. His creative connection to Scotland continued, in writing both the TV and radio series of *Dr Finlay's Casebook*.

To those who knew him, he was a human whirlwind, always working on a thousand projects whether paid and unpaid. In his home town, St Albans in Hertfordshire, he co-founded a still thriving theatre company and poetry society, and would regularly discomfort local councillors with popular petitions to save ancient trees and period buildings from the bulldozers. In his professional life he was a leading campaigner for Public Lending Right, and as an executive committee member of International PEN, campaigned energetically for writers imprisoned abroad. He also loved helping ambitious, young people get that first break into the television – one of whom was *Harry Potter* film producer Mike Newell.

When Arthur Swinson died in 1970, hundreds packed into St Albans Cathedral for his memorial service, unable to believe that this extraordinary, larger than life, driven, kindly personality had actually left town.

Cold, commercial logic in a world of commoditisation of both books and authors, would suggest that there is nothing quite so dead as a dead author. But thanks to the imaginative vision of Luath Press, Arthur Swinson lives on, in this remarkable book.

His talent also endures for the future: in the lives and potential of his two grandchildren, Rory and Ella Swinson Reid, to whom this new edition is dedicated.

Antonia Swinson
Edinburgh, November 2005

Antonia Swinson is an Edinburgh based journalist and writer. Her latest book *Root of All Evil?* is published by St Andrew Press.

Foreword

IT NATURALLY GIVES me great pleasure to write a foreword to Mr Arthur Swinson's dogged pursuit of the facts about the ss *Politician*, and in doing so to be able to testify to the accuracy with which he has told what everybody will surely find an absorbing tale.

There is only one question to which Mr Swinson has not given me an answer. Why were 20,000 cases of Scotch whisky shipped from Liverpool and how did they get there? I have been told that the Secretary of State for Scotland, the Rt Hon Thomas Johnston, after a lot of whisky was lost by enemy action in Glasgow and in Leith, decided that no more of the precious liquid should be wasted by German bombs and gave orders for all the whisky available to be immediately evacuated. At a Highland gathering in the late St Andrew's Hall after that great Scottish Secretary had been talking about hydro-electricity I told the audience that much as I admired his achievements over water I was even more grateful for his prompt action over whisky, thanks to which so many of his countrymen were able to enjoy, free of duty, their native spirit in the land that produced it.

And I take this opportunity of declaring that the destruction of so much of that whisky by the Customs and Excise adds one more example to the long and dreary record of bureaucratic hebetude. Cherishing as I do a deep regard and affection for those men and women of the West with whom I lived so happily for many years I am glad to be assured by Mr Swinson that a third of that cargo was salvaged by those who had a moral right to it whatever the law might say.

Two or three years ago as I was walking from Brook Street into Grosvenor Square a lorry pulled up by the zebra crossing.

I turned to acknowledge the courtesy as I always do and walked on. Presently I heard footsteps behind me and the driver of that lorry as he caught up with me looked round. 'Yes, I thought it *was* you,' he said. 'I was one of the crew of the *Politician*. We had a good deal of it but I expect you had more.'

And as I look back to perhaps a hundred bottles standing to attention along the top of my bookshelves I realize how right he was. I wish *Scotch on the Rocks* the success enjoyed by *Whisky Galore* for sixteen years.

Compton Mackenzie

The Song of the *Politician*

Don't ask me why I'm feeling sad,
   My thoughts are melancholy.
The truth is that I've had a dram
   Of whisky from the *Polly*.
For that's the ship that came ashore,
And you never saw her like before –
She'd whisky in the hold galore
   And it's led me into folly!

When they brought the news that she was there
   I took my boat to board her;
Found silk and cotton, sherry, stout,
   And fine goods ranged in order.
But down there in the flooded end
Was every kind of brand or blend
That God or a kindly fate could send –
   And me the first marauder!

'Twas clear to me and clear to all
   That ship was wrecked for ever;
And if we left the whisky there
   It would be tasted never.
But soon the Customs came around
And though I'd hid it underground
My stock of good 'Spey Royal' they found –
   And I thought I'd been so clever!

So to Lochmaddy Court I went,
    Bewildered and outwitted.
The Fiscal stood and read the charge
    But I would not admit it.
The policemen stood around there tense
While the Customs gave their evidence –
But the Sheriff said it didn't make sense
    And so I was acquitted!

So here's a health to the Captain bold
    Of the good ship *Politician*!
And here's to the rock she struck that night,
    A-sailing on her mission!
What's left of her can still be found
Off Calvay Isle in Eriskay Sound;
Of all great ships she is renowned –
    The *Polly*!
    The *Polly*!
        We shall not see her like again
        Though we live from now to a hundred and ten,
    The good ship *Politician*!!

Gaelic Ballad by Roddy Campbell
Translated by Norman MacMillan
English version by Arthur Swinson

CHAPTER I

A Ship Sails

AT 3.05 PM ON MONDAY, 3 February, 1941, a ship steamed gently out of Mersey harbour and headed west down the channel towards the open sea. Though there was a fresh breeze the day was overcast, and by the time she had reached the Bar Light Ship it was dark. The ship was the ss *Politician* (gross tonnage 7,939) and her orders were to sail to the north of Scotland and there rendezvous with a convoy. She was then to sail on to Jamaica and the United States of America.

Among seamen she was rated a good, sound ship with excellent crew accommodation. She was fast too for those days and could cruise at seventeen knots. It was her speed, in fact, that had decided that she should go north on her own; ships had been torpedoed in coastal waters, but for a ship like the *Politician* the risk was considered negligible. She had been built in 1923 by the Furness Ship Building Company, at Haverton Hill-on-Tees, in County Durham, designed for the Pacific trade; and for years she crossed and recrossed the oceans, bearing the name Sofss the ss *London Merchant*, the largest and fastest ship in the Furness Withy line. Then, in 1935, she was sold and renamed the *Politician* and set to work on the North Atlantic run. Four years later the war broke out and her bright peacetime colours were lost beneath the dull browns and greens of camouflage, as she became engaged in the arduous and often perilous business of saving Britain from starvation. But even in wartime she was a popular ship to sail in. 'With all those knots,' the men would say, 'you can get yourself out of trouble.'

Her Master, Captain Beaconsfield Worthington, was popular too. A Liverpudlian of 63, he had over forty years at sea behind him; and though he may have been a bit dour and humourless, no one was likely to hold that against him.

Frivolity is not a quality greatly admired on the Mersey, especially in sea captains, and in any case he was a man who got on with the job and did not throw his weight around too much. Off the bridge he could be sociable, convivial even. Sometimes he would drop in to see the Chief Engineer (Ted Mossman) or the Second Engineer (Tom Huntington) and drink with them in their cabins till three in the morning. He was not a stickler for detail, and for some tastes he could have glanced at the rule book rather more frequently; but no one would have denied that he was a good skipper, and he knew his job.

The Mate was Mr R A Swain, from Eastham in Cheshire. Though he was twelve years younger than Worthington, some of the crew noticed that he was beginning to look tired and strained. The Second Officer was Mr W P Baker of Liverpool; and the Third Officer Mr R H Platt of Penwortham, Preston. Also among the ship's complement, which totalled fifty-two, were two cadets: Maurice Watson and Fothergill Cottrell, both aged 17. It was Cottrell's first voyage, and as he watched the low banks of the channel move slowly past, his anticipation of the adventure to come was tinged with a slight feeling of homesickness and apprehension. He came from a seafaring family, his father being Commander V S Cottrell, RNR, and he had been trained for the sea at Pangbourne Nautical College in Berkshire. But now he was aboard his first ship and receiving his first orders; it was a day he would always remember.

'How's her head?'

'085 degrees, sir.'

'Keep her steady on that.'

'Aye, aye, sir.'

There was a company rule that in coastal waters the Captain should remain on the bridge. But rule or no rule, when a ship negotiates the Mersey channel, the Captain would not dare be anywhere else. Though the pilot gives the orders to the AB at the wheel, the responsibility for the ship is still his. The channel is long and tortuous; nowhere is it very wide and at its narrowest it is only twice the width of a football pitch. Apart from other ships, there are hazards such as floating wreckage, mudbanks which are constantly changing their contours, or buoys which have floated out of position. In heavy mist or fog, or in a high wind, the journey can be a nightmare; but even on a clear day there is no time to relax.

Mr Swain, the Mate, was glad of a rest on his bunk. He had been through an exacting forty-eight hours, for, apart from supervising the loading of the cargo, he had had to sign on the crew at the Board of Trade office. Luckily, on this voyage, only one man had failed to report – a fireman – but several were late, and getting all the forms completed and signed had taken some hours. (Later on in the war, the owners were to appoint an officer to do nothing else but look after crews, but in 1941 it was still the Mate's job.) Things had not been made any easier by the fact that the cargo included whisky – and some of the cases had been mysteriously damaged on their journey to the docks, or on the quayside as they awaited shipment. The bottles in the damaged cases, however, still remained whole, and, in their frequent breaks, the dockers could be seen pouring the neat spirit into their tea mugs and swilling it down. But despite such activities, the whole cargo, including bales of cotton, bicycles, machine tools and everything else was loaded on time.

The Captain's orders were to anchor for the night at the Bar and then steam north the following morning. As he went up on deck before breakfast he noticed that although the sky was still overcast the wind had freshened a little from the south east, but for February the going should be good. Sunset would be at 1755 hours (1655 GMT) giving him about ten hours of daylight to steam past the Isle of Man, across the Irish Sea, and out through the North Channel. As it happened, the night closed in early and the officer on watch did not see Rathlin Island, off the Irish coast, as the ship went by to the east; but he was not greatly concerned. Soon she was in the open sea and with the Atlantic waves beneath her, long and even, and quite different from the broken rhythms close in to shore. To a sailor the feeling of deep water comes almost as a benediction; he is not only safe, he is where he belongs.

Eight pm. The Third Officer, Platt, came on watch. There was no land till the Skerryvore Lighthouse, sixty miles to the north, and as long as he kept well to the seaward of it, there could be no trouble. At least he hoped not. But at 10 pm with the Skerryvore twenty miles off, the look-out on the bows sang out that there were ships steaming towards them. Summoned from his cabin, the Captain came up on the bridge immediately, and realized that his ship had come into the track of a large convoy. With no moon and with all side-lights dimmed it was not going to be easy to avoid a collision. But he had to go on – there was no alternative, for apart from the impossibility of anchoring, there was his RV with the convoy to consider. If he were late and it sailed without him, the wrath of his employers would descend upon him, not to mention the displeasure of their lordships at the Admiralty. So, carefully, he steered his course through the parallel lines of ships, observing when they zigzagged, and giving his orders to the helmsman accordingly. His men were watching him and he knew it; but his great experience of the sea had not let him down before, and would not now. In half an hour the last ships of the convoy and the inevitable stragglers had gone by to the south, and the crisis was over. Captain Worthington went back to his cabin and the *Politician* steamed north at seventeen knots.

Midnight. Baker came on watch. Though he had been sitting in a darkened cabin for twenty minutes to let his eyes become adjusted, he noticed immediately that the night was black; and the wind was blowing half a gale from the south east. But his watch passed without incident and at 4 am the Mate came up to relieve him. The ship was now passing the Skerryvore, well to the west, and heading for the wide entrance to the Minch, the channel between Skye and the Outer Hebrides. It was not a track the *Politician* would have used in peacetime, but with the German submarines attacking merchantmen wherever they could find them, all routing was in the hands of the Admiralty and ships had to go where they were told. Not that the Minch is a particularly difficult channel, except in very rough weather; at its narrowest it is fourteen miles across and for most of its 130 miles it is two or three times that width. Swain checked the ship's head, had a word with the AB at the wheel, and moved out to take observation from the starboard wing.

There had been several squalls during the night, and now the rain was coming down steadily, striking the white crests of the waves before they hurled themselves across the bows. The wind had begun to howl and though, according to the ship's chronometer, it was only an hour from first light, it might have been 2 am. The ship rolled and pitched in the blackness; but the orders were to keep going full steam ahead, and they had to be obeyed.

Suddenly there was a shout from the gunner on the starboard wing.

'Hard a port! Hard a port!'

Swain left the wheel and rushed across to him. 'What's up?'

The gunner gesticulated frantically: 'A battleship on the starboard bow, sir!'

The AB had swung the wheel over, but before the ship could answer there was a loud grating beneath the keel and a violent tremor that shook her from end to end. For what seemed an age she rode half out of the water, then the stern dropped down with a crash and she was motionless.

'Captain on the bridge!'

Worthington swung out of his bunk, grabbed some clothes and hurried up the stairs. Like most of the crew not on duty, he had been jerked out of his sleep by the crash and was moving instinctively, still half dazed. About him he could hear shouts and cries as men tried to find out what had happened and warn their mates. Down in the engine-room, Tom Huntington was on duty. After the first impact, he had heard something clattering against the side of the ship, and moved along to investigate. It was an electric fan. At first he thought that it had been swung out of position, but then to his horror he saw that the ship had been dented below the water-line for a length of six feet or more. He ran to the blower and put a call through to Mossman's cabin.

'Chief – would you come down, please?'

'I'm on my way.'

The Chief was not one to flap, but when the occasion demanded he could move as fast as anyone. He hurled himself out of the cabin, pushed his way past the men talking excitedly in the corridor and a few seconds later was down below.

Worthington had reached the bridge and was following Swain out on to the starboard wing. 'What the hell is it?' he was asking, his brain numbly aware that he had committed the unforgiveable sin of a Captain and let his ship run aground.

'A rock, sir.'

Peering through the rain and the darkness, the gale shrieking behind him, he could feel rather than see the great mass of rock facing him above the waves. For perhaps five seconds he stood motionless then he turned and strode back to the wheel.

'Full astern!'

'Full astern, sir.'

The telegraph tinkled and the reverberation from the engines shook the decks; but the ship did not budge. Motionless the Captain waited. . . thirty seconds. . . a minute. Then he barked:

'Full ahead!'

'Full ahead, sir.'

Again the throbbing power from the engines, but the ship remained motionless, almost as if she were held in the clutch of a giant hand. For all the power it had to urge her forward, the propeller might have been made of tissue paper.

Down in the engine-room, Mossman and Huntington were obeying the signals as they were transmitted from the bridge, though their engineering sixth sense told them they were useless. They were not even surprised when a fireman ran up, shouting, 'The water's coming in, sir!'

Mossman turned to him calmly: 'All right, I've seen it,' he said. 'Get back to your post.'

The water had been coming in since the moment of impact, silently, almost apologetically, but from two or three inches it had now risen to a foot. More than that. . . almost two feet.

'Full ahead!'

'Full astern!'

The telegraph kept tinkling as the Captain went on doggedly, trying to free his ship. But, watching the rising water-level, Mossman was getting anxious about his boilers. If an explosion was to be avoided the steam must be got out of them.

'Sir! Sir!' A deck hand came splashing towards him from the stern. 'It's no use!'

'What's no use?'

'The propeller shaft's been driven right up against the deck-head. It's broken right through.'

The firemen had gathered round now in a tight ring. Instinctively they glanced towards the boilers, then turned back towards Mossman to await his order. But he ignored them to speak to Huntington: 'Tom, ring the bridge. Finish with engines.'

Huntington hesitated a moment. This signal usually comes from the bridge, not the engine-room, but he went to the telegraph nevertheless. Meanwhile Mossman had detailed some men to shut off the fuel and help deal with the boilers; the others he dismissed, and they were soon scrambling up the ladders towards the relative safety of the decks.

On the bridge the officers stood silently, awaiting orders from the Captain. Cottrell was there too; he was due on watch at 8 am but now he was not quite sure whether he should stay. After a while he decided there was nothing he could do, and it would therefore be wiser to make himself scarce. But before leaving he had time to notice Swain, looking pale and rather shaken, as well he might. He had kept the ship on course – he was sure of it. Every time he had crossed the bridge, he had checked the heading and seen that the AB was doing his job properly. But where could they have got to? Barra Head should still be thirteen miles to the west; the islands of Rum and Eigg, thirty miles or more to the east. But there was that great rock out in front of them, and more rock holding them fast by the keel. Shocked, bewildered, he tried to grope for a solution.

Meanwhile Mossman had come up on the bridge and reported to the Captain. 'There's three feet of water in the engine-room, sir, and still rising. The shaft has snapped in two.'

Worthington nodded, numbly. A few minutes ago his ship had been sailing confidently at seventeen knots; now it was a wreck, and there was nothing he could do to save it.

'Have you got the pumps going?'

'Yes, Captain.'

'The bilge injection?'

'Yes, sir. They're all working.'

The Captain walked through to the chart-room, followed anxiously by Swain. The next thing was to work out their position and put out an sos. Though the ship was still motionless, it was being pounded heavily and there was a real danger that it would start to break up.

On deck, the crew were still groping about in the darkness, searching for information. Constantly they bumped into each other or tripped and barked their shins against the deck gear, and cursed. But curses, like orders, counter-orders, questions and answers, were all distorted and finally lost in the gale. The men knew that the ship now had a list, but whether she was sinking, or how fast, they had no idea. Stories came up from below that the engine-room was flooded, that the stern had been ripped off, but in the noise and confusion it was impossible to tell what was happening. Then, no one could afterwards say why, a shout was heard above the gale: 'Abandon ship! Lower the port boat!'

Cottrell heard this order and ran across to the davits. Here he found the carpenter, Mr Gillies, in charge and about twenty men clambering aboard the boat.

'Lower away.'

The boat was swung out on the davits and let down gently into the angry seas attacking the sides of the stricken ship. The carpenter ordered the men to take out the oars and start rowing; it was quite obvious that unless the boat was to be smashed to matchwood it must be got clear at once. But the painter was foul and all efforts to free it proved useless. Finally it had to be chopped in two with the boat axe.

All this took time; and before it was finished the men could hear voices hailing them from the ship and ordering them to return. What had happened was that the Captain, on sending for the carpenter, had been told that he had left with the boat. Immediately he rounded on Baker and asked him on whose authority he had given the order to abandon ship. Baker swore that he had given no such order and did not even know that a boat had been lowered. So the Captain sent him to get it back – an impossibility, as he soon discovered. Already the boat was clear and moving towards the bows of the ship. . . and then it was lifted by a giant wave, and disappeared into the darkness.

Meanwhile, the Radio Officer had begun tapping out his signals. 'SOS. Steamer *Politician*. Ashore south of Barra Island. Pounding heavily.' And later: 'SOS. Steamer *Politician*. Ashore south of Barra Island. Request immediate assistance.' No one knew how the Captain had come to decide that this was their position; but he seemed quite certain and no one dare raise any query. Fortunately, the signal was picked up by the coastguard on Barra, and also by the duty officer at the Royal Navy headquarters in Port Patrick. He signalled the nearest ship, HMS *Abelia*, who replied, quite reasonably:

'East or west of island? Cannot make west side till daylight.' But the duty officer could not tell him. The signal was also picked up by the duty officer at Lloyd's, London, and by the officer monitoring signals from foreign ships – in Berlin.

Meanwhile, the men in the boat were having a bad time of it. With the roughness of the water and the strength of the currents, all attempts at rowing proved ineffective; and in any case no one had any notion as to where the land lay. The only hope was to somehow keep the boat floating till daylight, which they knew could not be far off. But the chances did not seem very great; the waves were tossing the craft to and fro like an insignificant piece of flotsam. And, worse still, throwing it against the rocks which lay all around in the darkness. This went on for half an hour or more, and why the bottom remained intact no one could imagine. Then quite suddenly the current took charge and swept the boat broadside towards the shore. But before it was grounded, the keel crashed against a submerged rock, throwing the boat over and hurling the men out of their seats and headlong into the roaring surf. They choked and spluttered in the cold water, but they were all swimmers and they struck out for the beach which lay a few yards ahead of them. The cook and a junior engineer shipped so much salt water that they were in danger of going under, but luckily they were spotted, and the men on either side of them hauled them to safety. Mercifully only one man had been injured, his leg sliced right up to the thigh by a sharp rock. But the rest of the crew were frozen and soaked to the skin, their faces blue and their teeth chattering. The older men were still struggling to catch their breath.

It was now first light and the rain had ceased, but there was a thick mist, restricting visibility to a few yards. Cottrell carried out a quick reconnaissance, to find that they had landed on a small cove, hemmed in by what looked like a sheer cliff of black rock. While the carpenter and a couple of the younger men rescued what stores they could from the boat, which was now resting on its side in shallow water, Cottrell explored a path up the cliff to find a sheltered spot for them to rest. Soon the remainder of the party had joined him, two of the old men in bad shape and being carried. Fortunately the carpenter had been able to rescue a bag with blankets in, and as soon as the old men's clothes had been stripped off, they were wrapped in the blankets and given artificial respiration. After a while they came round, their breathing became regular, and the party began to organize itself.

Three men were sent off to reconnoitre the island and find out if it was inhabited. Cottrell and two sailors went off to collect driftwood for a fire. It was not difficult to find, though it was wet, and soon they had quite a pile. The carpenter scraped off the outside, split up the dry parts into convenient sizes, and quickly had a fire going. The men squatted round it gratefully, taking off their wet clothes, a garment at a time, to dry them, then putting them on again. They were hungry, and had no idea when they'd eat again. But they were alive – and far from being depressed.

Aboard the *Politician* the Radio Officer was still sending out the sos. Some ships replied, asking for his exact position, but he couldn't tell them. As an additional distress signal, the Captain had ordered the ship's siren to be sounded; but so far this had produced no results either. Possibly it didn't carry in the thick mist, or possibly there was no one close enough to hear it if it did. All that anyone aboard could say was that they were on the rocks and being pounded. . . and the sooner help came from some quarter, the better.

Actually, had they known it, the Barra lifeboat, *Lloyd's,* had been launched from Castlebay at 10 am and was heading south. A coastguard on the island of Eriskay who had picked up the *Politician*'s sos had signalled his headquarters at Kyle of Lochalsh, on the mainland. From there the message was relayed to the lifeboat secretary at Castlebay, who had telephoned the coxswain, Murdoch MacNeil.

In the great traditions of their service, the lifeboat crew went out in the gale to answer the sos from the *Politician* without hesitation, though they had little idea of where they might find her. Barra is not one island, but a whole group of islands stretching from Fiaray and Fuday in the north down through Barra itself, Vatersay, Sandray, Lingay, Pabbay, Mingulay, and Berneray with Barra Head at its southern tip. This is a journey of some twenty-two miles, and the rocky coastlines cover seven or eight times that distance. Also, the whole area is rendered more difficult by violent currents, shoals, sandbanks, and rocks. In fine weather the search would have been difficult enough, but in a heavy sea and with the mist swirling across the bows, not to mention the lack of precise information, the odds were almost impossible. The only real hope was that more information would come over the radio; but at the moment reception was bad.

Aboard the ship, things were slightly easier now. The wind had veered to the south and dropped slightly, and although the ship was still being pounded there seemed no immediate danger of her breaking up. Also, though the list was pronounced, general opinion was that it had not become any worse. In the absence of the carpenter, the Bosun had sounded round and reported that the engine-room and Nos. 5 and 6 holds were flooded, No. 1 hold was leaking slightly, and Nos. 2, 3 and 4 seemed to be watertight. The ship's siren was still sounding mournfully in the mist but no boats had appeared. Actually, it had been heard by the people on the islands to the north and the south, but it was difficult for them to decide where the sound was coming from. The Lloyd's agent, Donald Ferguson, was informed over the telephone that a ship was on the rocks, and tried to hire a boat to go out and find it; but the sea was too rough and no boat-man would take the risk. A coastguard who heard the siren phoned his headquarters at Kyle of Lochalsh. The information was passed to the lifeboat secretary who radioed the Barra lifeboat, now battling with the seas down by Barra Head. The signal was faint but could be read distinctly: it said that the *Politician* was not south of Barra, as stated in her SOS; she was in the Sound of Eriskay.

Murdoch MacNeil put the helm over and the lifeboat turned to begin the long journey north. It was not going to be very pleasant, and if the mist had not lifted by the time they reached Eriskay they would be in for real trouble. As he knew only too well, the Sound was shallow and guarded by rocks, some of them like the red rocks of Hartamul, pointing their savage blades above the water, and others even more dangerous, lurking just beneath the surface. To make matters worse, it would be getting on for low water.

At three o'clock, the fire which had been comforting the men ashore began to run out of fuel and Cottrell offered to go down to the beach again with a radio operator and collect a fresh supply. While he was there he spotted a tin of biscuits floating at the edge of the water, and rescued it. If the party were marooned much longer, it might help keep them alive, for the parties reconnoitring the island had already come back to report that there were no signs of habitation. All they could find was rock, peat, and a few wandering sheep. The men were resigned to spending the night in the open, and some said the mist might linger on for days. Then suddenly, to everyone's surprise, it vanished, almost it seemed in a matter of seconds. Cottrell, his arms loaded with wood, looked up to see that he was standing on a large hilly island, with houses dotted about in the distance.

'Look – the ship!'

The radio operator was pointing excitedly to the *Politician,* which lay less than three hundred yards away. Facing it was a small islet about a hundred yards across, set slightly to the near side of a channel. This must have been the 'battleship' that the gunner saw in the night. Around the *Politician* was a collection of small craft which had somehow found it through the mist. But what fixed Cottrell's attention was the extraordinary position into which the ship had managed to place herself. Apart from the land on either side of the channel, which he judged to be about half a mile wide, and the islet ahead, there were sandbanks and rocks in a ring behind her. How she had come straight through them at seventeen knots, he could not imagine. Also, her head was pointing up the channel – that is north west or even north west by west. How was this to be explained? As far as he knew the course up the Minch lay ten or more points to the east. It was possible that the ship had swung after the impact; but unless she had been travelling west how could she have reached the present position at all?

Captain Worthington was equally mystified. When the fishermen had come aboard an hour earlier, the first thing he had asked them was his position. When they told him he was between Eriskay and South Uist, he had gone to the chartroom and run his finger up the long skein of islands which make up the Outer Hebrides; and when he saw his position on the chart he was rather shaken. Swain felt almost too ill and sick to speak. As a brother officer said later: 'He looked like a broken man.' But to give him credit, he made no attempt to evade or diminish his responsibility. 'It was my fault,' he said. 'Completely my fault.' Later on he gave Cottrell and Watson, the two cadets, a tin of toffees to share between them. He said: 'I'm sorry that you should be involved in an incident like this at the beginning of your careers. Perhaps from now on you'll have better luck. I certainly hope your careers won't be ended as sadly as mine.'

Worthington was still concerned about the carpenter and the party ashore. Till reports reached him (after the mist had lifted) that they could be seen waving from the cliffs, he had expected that many of them would be drowned. Now he asked some of the fishermen to take a boat to Eriskay and bring the men back on board. Half an hour later they arrived, in good spirits but expecting a reprimand for leaving the ship in the first place. But the Captain was preoccupied with other things. He merely told them to go to their cabins, collect up their belongings, and prepare to abandon ship again.

Soon after 4 pm the Barra lifeboat arrived, after six hours at sea. Already the light was beginning to fade, and the coxswain was anxious to get the crew off without delay. Worthington ordered the Radio Officer to signal: 'Steamer *Politician*. Abandoning ship.' Then, starting with the young cadets, the crew went over the side on the rope ladder and clambered aboard the lifeboat. Worthington, one of the lifeboatmen noticed, looked dazed, though by contrast some of the men were in remarkably good spirits. At first he thought that this was due to their relief at getting away from the ship, but then he noticed that many of them had whisky bottles protruding from their pockets. The bottles were also spotted by the islanders when, after a long and uncomfortable journey, the lifeboat reached Castlebay soon after 8 pm. Here the crew were split up into small parties and billeted in the crofts whose hospitable owners offered them clothing, a hot meal and a bed. But, like all islanders, the people of Barra are insatiably curious about ships, especially those wrecked off their shores; and after supper questions were asked, politely but persistently. What was the ship called? Where had it come from? Where was it going? How had it got itself into Eriskay Sound? And then, almost as an afterthought: *What had it got aboard?*

The crew, feeling the warmth of the peat fires and the comfort of the meal inside them, and with the prospect of a soft bed for the night, were in no mood to be churlish. If their hosts wanted to know about the ship, who were they to withhold information? The chances were, anyway, that they'd never see it again. 'What's aboard her?' they said. 'Whisky – twenty thousand cases of it!'

So in the crofts of Barra there began the most extraordinary story ever to come out of the Western Isles; a story that within a few years was to become a legend, known all over the world; a story that was to inspire a Gaelic ballad, a novel, and a film; a story whose origins, so most people believed, were irretrievably lost in the Celtic mists.

This book is an account of my attempt to uncover the story,

and to trace the people who were involved in it. Where possible, I have tried to separate the fact from the legend, though at times this has been difficult, if not impossible. But even where only the legend remains, I have thought it worth recounting, not just for its own sake but because I believe that all legends are true – in their own way. Anyone violently disagreeing with this premise is invited to read the life of Heinrich Schliemann and the discovery of Troy.

It may be asked – as it was often as I travelled about on my research – why the story of the *Politician* is still of such great interest, now the whisky is all drunk and the ship itself no longer exists. To that I reply that the whisky is by no means all drunk; and the ship has become more famous in its death than it ever was in its life. But more important still is the fact that this story happened to the right people and at the right time. In a chaotic world this does not happen often; and when it does, it should be recorded.

CHAPTER 2

Quest in the Hebrides

THE FIRST TIME I heard about the *Politician* was in 1943. I was Staff Captain to the 5th Infantry Brigade in the 2nd Division and we were stationed in a desolate spot called Galunche, about thirty miles up in the hills above Poona. The Brigade consisted of the 1st Cameron Highlanders, the 2nd Dorsetshires, and my own battalion, the 7th Worcestershires; the Brigade Headquarters contained men from all three of these distinguished regiments, many of them chuck-outs. In addition to the chuck-outs there were some good soldiers (officers and men) who for some reason had not seen eye to eye with their commanding officers and had been removed at the first opportunity. (Fortunately, for the purposes of this story, it is not necessary to allocate myself to either category.)

Poona was not then an exciting town, and from what I can gather it has not improved much since; but after the barren wastes of Galunche, it seemed almost a paradise. My occasional trip down there, to sort out such exciting matters as the local rates for sweepers (wet and dry), the *dhobi* charges for shirts khaki, or, more occasionally, the psychiatrist's report for a court martial, made the high spot of the week. Occasionally a brother officer would discover some urgent necessity to visit his bank or his *dhurzi* and come along with me. We would make our way to the Poona Club and drink several gins before a heavy lunch, or, if he happened to be a member, enjoy the rather more splendid surroundings of the Club of Western India, with its large billiard-room. On one particular trip the driver was a Jock, a somewhat taciturn character whose name, as far as I can remember, was

MacNeil. He drove at a steady pace, somehow managing to avoid the jay-walkers, the beggars seated on the edge of the roadway, and the ubiquitous *bail-garis*, though not without some desperately narrow shaves. We were about half-way to Poona before he opened his mouth to remark briefly: 'There's been some strange things happening in the islands.'

Politely I asked him which islands; my geography in those days not being what it might be.

'The Hebrides. They're saying a boat's gone ashore with a load of whisky aboard. Thousands of bottles.'

He drove on past another village and through a long tunnel of banyan trees before adding: 'Thousands of them.'

I had never visited the Hebrides, indeed I had never been to Scotland at all, and the exact significance of the remark escaped me. But, watching his face as he drove, I could see that the events had made a great impression on him, and though his eyes were intent on the road, his mind was back home in the islands. Probably he was suffering at the thought of that vast quantity of whisky pouring down thousands of throats; but he did not say any more, and before long we were in Poona and steering a course towards the street of the *dhurzis*. After that day, although I stayed with the Brigade till early 1945, I never saw him again.

It must have been in 1950, I suppose, that I picked up Compton Mackenzie's novel, *Whisky Galore*, and read in the foreword that his ss *Cabinet Minister* had no connection with 'the ss *Politician* which ran aground in the Outer Hebrides'. Immediately my mind went back to MacNeil. This was the incident he'd been talking about – this was the story which had transported him in a flash from the heat of India to the cold winds of the Western Isles! I enjoyed the novel immensely, and the film which was made from it; but at the back of my mind lay a whole host of queries. What had really happened? How had the ship got among the islands in the first place? Was there really that amount of whisky? Was there a battle with the authorities; and if so, who had won it?

By the early fifties I was fairly well established as a documentary writer; and sometimes over a lunch-time beer in the old Rose of Normandy I would hear Scottish writers such as Duncan Ross or Robert Barr speak of the *Polly*, as she was now called. Anecdotes would be bandied about, some of them very amusing, but there seemed no means of checking them or tracking them down to their source, let alone setting them in a framework of fact. When Sir Compton Mackenzie began coming to the studios for his memorable series *The Glory that was Greece*, I determined to beard him the first time we met. But we never did meet, and in 1961 I left the BBC to work as a free-lance.

One of my first jobs was to investigate the possibility of a series on the work of Her Majesty's Customs and Excise, and, as I must admit, I approached it with some apprehension.

So far as I knew no writer up to then had got into the Customs and come out alive again with any usable material. But to my delight the people there turned out most helpful; and before I had even fathomed the difference between customs and excise, plans were already in hand to take me on a tour of the ports, the Irish Land Boundary, and the whisky distilleries up on Speyside. My guide was Maurice Nockles, the Press Officer, and we had a delightful week. On the way back there were a few hours to spare between planes and Nockles took me into the Custom House at Glasgow to visit the Collector (which means the senior official of a region) and introduce me to some of his old friends. One of these, after the initial courtesies were over, held up a battered-looking file, asking: 'I've got the *Whisky Galore* file here. What the hell should I do with it?'

Nockles, to my relief, replied: 'Send it to me. I'd like to read it.'

I knew the rule about Customs documents – that they could not be released for fifty years – but flying down to Manchester I decided to broach the subject. Here, for the first time, was tangible proof that the *Politician* had existed. Nockles was friendly, but non-committal. 'You can make an application,' he said. 'The Commissioners might consider it favourably.'

Through pressure of work on the pilot script for the Customs series, I did not get round to making an application, but two months later when I happened to be in Nockles's office, he remarked casually: 'I've had an American in to see me about the *Politician*. He's been up to the islands with a tape-recorder and wants to do a radio programme.' I smiled somewhat wryly. While I had been thinking about the subject, someone else had leaped in and got ahead of me. But later on the American (whose name I discovered was Miller) turned out to be no rival but a benefactor. Somehow he had persuaded the Customs to release photostats of about thirty documents; and when I put in my application the same documents were made available to me. Afterwards, in March, when my researches began in earnest, Miller seemed to stride ahead of me like a ghost. Having pursued the most involved and tenuous lines of inquiry, I would be informed by the man I vainly imagined could help me: 'You're too late. Miller's been here.' Though such experiences were annoying, I was nevertheless saved a good deal of time: explanations as to what I required were not necessary, and files had already been ransacked. It took me six weeks or more before I could lose the ghost of Miller entirely. He had not been over here long, but he had certainly moved.

One morning I received a telephone call from HM Customs to say that the photostats were ready for collection, the fee being a very reasonable one of £5. Soon they were in my possession, the first documents I could take home and study. They consisted of reports from Charles McColl, the Officer at Lochboisdale, and from Ivan Gledhill, the Surveyor at Portree who was his superior. (Perhaps I should explain here that in the Outdoor Service of the Customs, Surveyor is the rank between Officer and Collector.) They were clear, beautifully-phrased reports, containing a mass of detailed information which would become of great use to me in due course. But at this stage the reports had certain defects. To begin with, they had been written for a special purpose and from a definite viewpoint; and they presumed a detailed knowledge of life in the islands which, so far, I did not possess. However, I was able to establish the exact date and site of the accident and the size of the cargo; 22,000 cases, each containing twelve bottles. But how much the islanders had got hold of, and how much was recovered, I still had to find out.

Leaving the reports for a while, I decided to concentrate my efforts on the question of the ship. From past experience I knew that anything and everything connected with the sea was clogged with mystery; that there was an invisible but effective barrier to keep strangers (that is non-seafaring people like myself) away from secrets which did not concern them.

So I started with the Historical Records section at the Admiralty with whom I had made contact some years previously when I was writing about Peter Heywood, the midshipman on the *Bounty*. They could not help me at all. (Later they did unearth a couple of signals, but that was all.) I went on to the Ministry of Transport, who are usually most helpful, but all they could say was: 'We've had an American asking the same question. . . but we couldn't find anything for him.' I pressed them saying that there must have been an inquiry of some sort, but they seemed quite certain that there had not been. So far, no progress at all.

Fortunately, a branch of my family is in shipping and from them I was able to learn about the Registrar General of Shipping and Seamen who has an office in Dock Street, in the East End of London. A telephone call to this office drew the information that the Ship's Log and papers would be stored in the Registrar General's office at Llandaff, Cardiff, but that if I cared to send the sum of four shillings they would be sent to Dock Street where I might inspect them. I dispatched a postal order immediately, but meanwhile rang Lloyd's, London, and spoke to an official of their Information Department. Non-committal, but at least not despondent, he promised to look into matters. Before I heard from him, however, an advice had come from the Registrar General and I went off to find Dock Street. Like most institutions connected with the sea, it was located in a grim, half-derelict area, and it was not in Dock Street at all, but in an even grimmer road running parallel, called Ensign Street. But the important thing was that the log was there, waiting for me to study it.

On the whole, it was disappointing. There was not as much information as I had hoped, and the entry concerning the accident was laconic in the extreme. The date was given as 5.2.1941. 7.45 am (approx.)'. The column headed 'Place of Occurrence, or situation by Latitude and Longitude at sea' was significantly left blank. The 'Date of Entry' column had 10.2.1941 written in. (Which meant five days after the accident.) The final column 'Entries required by Act of Parliament' had this:

'Vessel grounded, damaging bottom and flooding engine-room. 4.45 pm. RN lifeboat took crew off for safety during the night.'

> Signed: B Worthington, Master.
>
> R A Swain, Mate.

And that was all. However, on other pages were set out the names, ages, and home addresses of the officers and crew:

B Worthington	Master. Age 63.
R A Swain	Mate. Age 51.
W P Baker	2nd Officer. Age 38.
R H Platt	3rd Officer. Age 26.
E H Mossman	Chief Engineer. Age 55.
T Huntington	2nd Engineer. Age 46.

My attention was specially drawn by two entries at the bottom of the crew list:

Cadets
Maurice Watson. Age 17.
Fothergill S Cottrell. Age 17.
(First Voyage.)

There were also some technical details of the ship:

Official Number: 147482.
Registered: Liverpool.
Tonnage: Gross: 7939.
Nett: 5047.
Departed Liverpool: 3 February, 1941. 3.5 pm.

The next thing, evidently, was to try and trace some of the officers. A clerk volunteered the information that if I applied to Llandaff, the Registrar General would forward letters to the last known address. But he also recommended that I contact the Merchant Navy and Airline Officers Association, Whitechapel High Street. I did so the same day, to receive this reply: 'I am sorry to inform you that none of the officers you have named are at present members of the Association. However, it is possible that one or more of them are now in command and may, therefore, be members of the Mercantile Marine Service Association, 6 Rumford Place, Liverpool 3.' I wrote this organization, with results which will be recounted later; but meanwhile, my attention had been centred on the cadet, Fothergill S Cottrell. The name, coupled with the address: 'Jumps House, Churt, Farnham, Surrey' seemed to indicate he came from a family of some substance which could be traced without too much difficulty. I began inquiries at the local post office, to be told that the family were no longer in the district; but a letter to the editor of the *Farnham Herald* produced the suggestion that Admiral Sir William James of Fife, Scotland, might prove helpful. I wrote to the Admiral, who replied by return, suggesting that a letter to Mrs Hamilton of Churt might produce the information. Mrs Churt replied that as far as she knew Fothergill was in Kenya, but she could give me his mother's last known address in the Isle of Wight. I wrote off to Mrs Cottrell, and had an immediate reply: her son was back from Kenya and had a strawberry farm near her, in the Isle of Wight. Also, he had written a long account of the voyage and the accident in the Hebrides, and if I would like it she would try and find her copy. Progress at last! I wrote off again, to Fothergill Cottrell, saying that I would like to come down and see him. He too replied by return – I have never known such a reliable set of correspondents in my life – saying he would be delighted to see me.

While I was pursuing this long though profitable trail, there were other interesting developments. Mr Dickens, the Head of the Information Department at Lloyd's, had produced the text of all signals received from the *Politician*, from the Lloyd's Agent at Lochboisdale and from the Liverpool and Glasgow Salvage Association. The signals dealt with a whole range of matters, starting with the SOS and going on to the efforts to save the ship and the cargo. Important too, they assigned events to specific dates. Immediately on receipt of these documents I rang up the

Liverpool and Glasgow Salvage Association to be told by a dour Liverpudlian voice that there were no records of the operation. The voice added, before ringing off: 'We told the American the same thing.' The Royal National Lifeboat Institution were far more courteous and helpful, sending me the official account of the rescue. Later, at my urgent request, they put me in touch with Angus MacDonald, the mechanic on the lifeboat, who in due course was to give me a whole mass of material. But to return to the signals themselves, the first thing which struck me was the SOS. In this the *Politician* kept giving her position as 'South of Barra'. Why should she imagine she was there, when in fact she was north of Eriskay? This was another thing I must start trying to fathom.

From the Mercantile Marine Service Association came news that Captain Worthington was dead, also the Second Officer, Baker, and the Chief Engineer, Mossman. They had, however, traced the Second Engineer, Huntington, who was living in North Wales, near Holywell, and would be glad to see me. I could not help reflecting that it was strange that my quest for the *Politician* should lead me to the same remote spot to which the quest for Corvo had led A J Symons. As it turned out, Huntington lived some miles from Holywell at a mountain village called Rhes-y-Cae, and as soon as I could make arrangements I motored up to see him. It was from the material that I obtained from Huntington, Cottrell, and MacDonald of the lifeboat crew that I was eventually able to reconstruct the events up to the time of the accident, as recounted in the previous chapter.

But that is leaping ahead somewhat. Before I had met any of these three, there came a point in my researches when I decided that if I were to really absorb and understand the material now becoming available through my exertions, let alone evaluate it, I must fly up to the Outer Hebrides. I must study the setting of the story, and as many of the people as I could find who were involved in it; and the sooner the better.

To reach the Outer Hebrides by air you fly to Glasgow, then board a plane for Stornoway, Benbecula, or Barra. My objective was Lochboisdale on South Uist, it being the nearest place to Eriskay with an hotel, and so I booked for Benbecula. My telegram to the hotel had produced a phone call from the manager who told me that the whole building was crawling with plumbers, electricians, builders, plasterers, and heaven knows what else, but that if I did not mind such inconveniences and could bring myself to eat with the staff, I could have a room. He also informed me that there was a causeway between Benbecula and South Uist and a road running straight the way down, but to make sure that I had no difficulty he would send a car to meet me at the airport. (Perhaps I should mention that neither the travel agent nor the AA could tell me how I got off Benbecula, an inquiry clerk at the latter remarking vaguely: 'I dare say there'll be a ferry.')

It was a glorious day, Friday 13 April. It had to be that day, as only on Friday the 13th were there any seats available on the plane. Leaving London at 6.30, I was in Glasgow for an early breakfast, and boarded the plane for Benbecula just before nine o'clock. The journey lay over the Western Highlands and though we climbed to something like twenty thousand feet we could look down through the clear, sparkling air at the brown foothills of the Grampians, then the Firth of Lorne, and beyond it, the Isle of Mull. The Captain of the aircraft, a bearded character and something of a wag, came up on the speaker to announce: 'Ladies and gentlemen, we are now passing Rum. By that I do not mean that the crew and myself are drinking, but that the island of Rum is now ahead of us, to starboard.' A few passengers gave a half-hearted snigger and we flew on over the lonely isle of

Canna, skirted the south western finger of Skye, and headed over the blue waters of the Minch. Soon a long, brown strip of land came up over the horizon: the Outer Hebrides. The plane veered a few points to port and headed straight for Benbecula, which we reached in what seemed a matter of minutes. The plane came down on the runway with a barely perceptible bump and we taxied to a halt, dead on time.

The airport buildings at Benbecula are little more than a collection of wooden huts, and as no car seemed to be waiting for me I went inside to inquire if there was a message. There was none, but the girl at the desk volunteered the information that there was a bus outside which would be leaving for Lochboisdale in less than ten minutes. I got aboard along with a dozen other people who were talking to each other spiritedly in a language I took to be Gaelic. Among them was a formidable though courteous lady I knew later as Miss Shand, manageress of the Highland Industries shop. There was also a real beauty of a girl with jet-black hair and a pale skin, wearing a university scarf. She spoke to her mother in English while her mother replied in Gaelic, but they both seemed happy with the arrangement. The driver was loading up with bundles of newspapers which he jammed into the racks above our heads. The outside papers were inevitably torn but this did not seem to worry him. What he could not get into the racks he stacked up in a pile by the driver's seat, and soon we began the journey south.

By English standards the road was rough and narrow, but, as I was soon to discover, no English or indeed any other foreign standards applied here. Not that this worried me. I had come not to moralize but to explore and to understand. But nevertheless the scenery was so strange, so different to anything I had seen before in Europe, Africa, or Asia, that I found myself reacting to it strongly; in fact it was some time before I could use my eyes with sufficient objectivity to attempt an accurate description. I realized then what Alasdair Alpin MacGregor meant when he wrote: 'The stranger to these islands is either attracted to them or repelled by them. He will either love them intensely or hate them intensely; he will never be merely indifferent to them.' But as the bus clattered south, I was in no condition to experience any such pure emotion; I was too confused.

The initial impact of the Hebridean scenery comes, I imagine, from the complete absence of trees and bushes, also the lack of reds and yellows. Rock abounds everywhere, sometimes rearing itself up into knolls or even small mountains, sometimes skirmishing along the ground in great slabs, or diminishing into scree or miniature boulders. Where the rock allows, lie areas of peat, running to a depth of seven feet or more, and covered with coarse, dull-green grass. And challenging the land, whether rock or peat, is the water; sea lochs, freshwater lochs, fjords, pools, skerries. Surely nowhere, not even in the Louisana swamps, is there such an intimate and delicate interplay of land and water. Sometimes, as we travelled on, the sea would retreat for miles to be lost over the horizon, sometimes it would hover a few yards off, either to left or right, and then it would swoop down on both flanks, only denied complete victory by the narrow causeway supporting the road. This situation would continue for a hundred yards or more, then without warning the sea would give up the struggle and banish itself back to the horizon. The established pattern of rock, peat, and loch would then return for some miles until the sea had gathered strength for its next onslaught.

Dotted among the rocks were the crofts, stone houses with sloping walls, rounded at the ends, and thatched roofs. Each croft stood on its own like an isolated fortress, usually without outbuildings or walls or fences to protect it. In England, and in most other countries, one is accustomed to seeing a whole variety of buildings; not only houses, but shops, factories, barns, churches, libraries, restaurants, hotels and cafés. But here there was only one kind of building, the croft, and I found myself wondering how the people organized their lives, where they went shopping, went to school, or sought entertainment. Farther on we did, in fact, reach what I took to be a village – a cluster of some dozen or more houses by the roadside, a dismal little shop, a post office, and what proved to be a pub. Outside the latter were parked half a dozen cars, which caused Miss Shand to exclaim: 'Look at all that traffic!'

All the way down, as the bus reached a road junction, the driver would hurl a bundle of newspapers out through the window. Usually there would be no one about, and I fell to wondering how long the papers would have to wait till their owner chanced upon them, that is if they had not disintegrated under the wheels of successive cars and lorries. But when I glanced back through the rear window of the bus I could see that someone had materialized out of the landscape and was already rescuing them. (I learned later it is the custom for anyone finding a parcel by the roadside to take it as far on its journey as he happens to be going, then dump it again. Thus it may pass through several pairs of hands – all working independently – before reaching its destination.) At one stop, the black-haired beauty and her mother got out with a large suitcase and began walking down a side road. As there were no houses in sight and the girl wore shoes which would have passed for high in Oxford Street I wondered what the chances were of her reaching home. Apparently she succeeded, as after lunch she arrived at the hotel with her father in a car, still with her high heels on and looking as fresh as ever. In the days that followed I got used to seeing people in city garb, walking great distances along the exposed roads of the island; and I decided that whether or not the writ of the law ran strong here, the writ of the women's magazines was undisputed.

We were now on South Uist, and far away to the east running parallel with the road was a range of mountains: Sheaval, Arnaval, Stalaval, and Truarebheinn, all bare, dun, and uninviting. The sea had vanished completely, but as a reminder that it was not far off it had left whole strings of lochs and pools. Also, menacing us from above was a great company of seabirds, too many and varied for me to identify.

The crofts were becoming more sophisticated, and there were even some pleasant Norwegian-type houses which, someone remarked, were being put up by the Inverness-shire County Council. There were also more cars and trucks on the road, the drivers halting at the passing bays or going on, as if controlled by radar. This was the first example I saw of the incredible ability of the islanders to divine each others' intentions without even the need for a signal. At first I thought it came from some strange gift akin to telepathy, but gradually came to realize that it was rather a matter of knowledge. Everyone on the islands knows the movements of everyone else, rather like dancers in a ballet.

Towards midday we came to what looked like a veritable town – Daliburgh. There were two churches, a Co-op, and a hundred houses or more, and even a poster announcing a film show. The bus swung round to the left and headed down the last few miles of road to Lochboisdale. There was a rise as we entered the place, and it was not until the bus had halted in a wide open space by the harbour that I could glimpse the Loch itself. The sun was shining – as it had been since I had left London – and as I collected my bag and tape-recorder and prepared to hump them across to the hotel, I just had time to glance at the wide blue channel and the islands lying peacefully towards the horizon. It was twelve o'clock.

The Lochboisdale hotel is a pleasant-looking building, perched up on a rise to the left of the harbour. As I reached the entrance hall, the manager bustled in from the dining-room; an upright, red-faced character, with a military moustache. At this moment he was complaining to a waitress that one of the maids was 'idle', but, seeing me, he came across and shook hands. After a polite greeting, I mentioned that the car I was expecting had not arrived, and so I had come down on the bus. 'Oh, that's all right,' he replied. 'I found I hadn't got one free today – but I knew you'd be all right.' This, considering that the journey was over twenty miles and he had suggested the car in the first place, I thought rather calm, but fortunately I held my peace, as he continued: 'You're after stories about the *Politician*, aren't you? I've got the very man here – Angus John Campbell. Dump your bags and I'll take you round.'

I followed him to a dingy, rather nondescript bar where a dozen or so cloth-capped men were drinking silently. He pointed to a man in the far corner and said, 'That's Angus,' then turned and walked out again. Diffidently, I moved over and introduced myself. He was a short man with wide shoulders and the face of a comedian, and having listened to me politely, he looked up and asked: 'The *Polly*? What would you be wanting from me?'

'Any stories you might care to give me.'

'Well, I dare say I could give you some. I gave plenty to the American.'

'Miller, you mean?'

'Aye, that's the man.'

Good old Miller, I thought. Still charging ahead of me, blazing the trail. 'When would it be convenient for you?' I asked Angus John.

He reflected for a moment, as if he had many plans of great complexity on his mind. Then he looked up and smiled. 'Should we say seven o'clock?'

'Seven o'clock,' I agreed, delighted. I bought him a pint of ale and went round to the front of the hotel, collected my baggage, and unpacked before lunch.

Before leaving London I had been given the address of Mrs McColl, the widow of Charles McColl, the Customs Officer who was an important figure in the story of the *Politician*, and after lunch I set off to find her. Her home was in one of the Norwegian-type houses, grouped in a rough crescent; but apparently she was out. However, the next-door neighbour put her head out of the window to say that she was down at the post office with her sister. So I retraced my steps, to be told by the postmistress, rather dour but not uncourteous, that she would send for Mrs McColl. I had just about time to reflect that this was probably the dingiest post office in the British Isles, when Mrs McColl arrived, a large and rather forbidding woman. I explained my business and arranged to see her the following afternoon. She was not enthusiastic, but at least she was not hostile, and reasonably content with my progress so far I walked along to the garage to see about hiring a car.

The *garagiste* (as the French would call him) was a civil, likeable man who agreed to let me hire a self-drive car the following afternoon. Meanwhile, if I wished, there was a truck with driver available. Gladly I accepted this offer, as there was a man over at South Lochboisdale I wanted to see, called Peter MacInnes. Angus John had mentioned his name as having been out at the *Polly*. We drove to Daliburgh, turned south for a mile or more, then headed east again till we found Peter's house near the edge of the loch. The driver, a handsome lad called Allan, came to introduce me, and I looked round for somewhere to set up my tape-recorder. Seeing this, Peter MacInnes laughed: 'It's no use here – we're on gas.' So I put the machine away and took up my notebook, while MacInnes sat by the fireplace opposite me. He was a lean old man with a great sense of humour, and he only had to cast his mind back to the *Polly* to begin shaking with laughter, 'What d'you want to know?' he roared. 'What the hell d'you want to know?' Then, more seriously: 'You're not from the Government, are you?'

Giving an immediate assurance, I said I wanted to know the whole story of the *Polly* from the islanders' point of view. How they knew the whisky was there. How they got out to it. How many of them were caught, and what happened to them. How much whisky was brought ashore, and what happened to that. Everything that had happened in the islands as a consequence of this great event. After a little prompting, he told me all he knew, but this was nothing like as much as I had expected, and it was lacking in detail. He had certainly been out to the wreck, but the whole story had merged in his old mind to a golden memory without clear outlines. Still he did give me a few useful things and I was grateful to him.

On the way back to Lochboisdale we picked up two plumbers who had been working on the new council houses near Daliburgh. They were talkative men from Lewis who told me that they preferred the country up there, but adding: 'There's no work for us there though. . . no work at all.' They asked me where I came from.

'St Albans, Hertfordshire,' I said. 'That's twenty miles north of London.'

They nodded, as if they knew Hertfordshire well, then asked: 'What's it like there? Is there plenty of work?'

'Yes,' I said. 'Plenty for everyone.'

They spoke of work as no one has spoken of it in England since the dark days of the depression, in the early thirties. The affluent sixties had obviously not yet reached Lewis.

Back at the hotel, I wandered into the cocktail bar, where two men I had seen at lunch were already drinking. 'You're late,' said one of them, whose name I gathered was Wilson. They open here at five.' Apologizing for my slackness and promising it would not happen again, I accepted a beer. Before I had time to start it Wilson had introduced his friend, who turned out to be Colonel Charles Cameron, brother of the Cameron of Lochiel, a quiet-spoken man but with an air of authority. This meeting (although I did not realize it then) was to have a great effect on my future research. But at this moment we talked of the Cameron Highlanders and the 1st Battalion which I had known out in Burma. It was obvious that every detail of the regiment and its history was of absorbing interest to him, and soon we were discussing Kohima and the subsequent battles on the long march to Imphal. By 6.30 we were so deep in the thickets of military history that it took an imperious summons from the gong to extract us.

They did not serve dinner at the hotel, but that Scottish abomination called high tea, which we ate seated on either side of a long table. The Colonel had an engagement so left smartly, but Wilson and I lingered on, soon to be joined by a charming, aristocratic-looking girl who told us she was a Technical Officer with the Ministry of Agriculture. With some vets she had been over to jab the cattle, and was now waiting to get her truck back on board the steamer. Between stories of her job, most of them very diverting, she glanced through the window to see if it were coming in.

Angus John was also waiting for the boat when I found him in the bar at seven o'clock. He told me as we drank that there were two men I must see: Neil Campbell and John Patterson, and I was just making a note of their names when there came the first blast of the steamer's siren. Immediately Angus John became restive. When I suggested that we go round to my room and record, he did not refuse but gave me to understand that he would be required on the quayside. Nor did my tentative suggestion that we should record later that night meet much approval. He said: 'I suppose you couldn't make it tomorrow night?'

'Of course. That's fine. I'll be here several days yet.' The steamer was now tied up alongside the jetty, and we left the bar and walked down towards it. The sun had gone down but the sky was clear and a diffused light turned everything to silhouette. The passengers were filing down the gangway, some to be greeted by friends or relations, and others wandering off alone. All around stood groups of islanders, their eyes on the boat. The girls were dressed up to kill, and with the subdued conversation they seemed to infuse the whole scene with an air of expectancy. Angus John was drifting around, having a word here and a joke there, though not attempting anything that would normally be described as 'work', and before long he disappeared with a friend from the crew in the general direction of the bar. The wind was cold now, coming off the sea, and I regretted not bringing my coat down with me. While I was debating with myself whether it was worthwhile going to the hotel to fetch it, the ship began taking on trucks, cars, and miscellaneous items of cargo, among them the truck belonging to the girl from the Ministry of Agriculture, whom I caught sight of farther along. From time to time officers would appear on deck and come down the gangway to have a quiet word with someone, nod briefly, and go back on board again. But nothing else happened, except that the islanders still stood around in the twilight, gazing at the ship, as if she were some sort of symbol. I began to think they would stay there till they froze, but suddenly, as if someone had given a signal in the darkness, they drifted away, leaving the ship silently moored against the jetty. The ritual, if ritual it had been, was over.

The receptionist at the hotel was a charming red-head called Jean, whom, later on, I got to know fairly well. She had been with a film unit out in Corsica, doing a continuity job, and hoped to rejoin it later for an epic to be shot in Africa. In the meantime she was working in Lochboisdale, but when I asked her why she had chosen such a remote spot, she refused to be drawn, remarking amiably: 'Well. . . it's quieter than Oxford Street.' But now she was looking up the telephone numbers of Neil Campbell and John Patterson and putting me through on the office phone. Fortunately they were both at home, though that was about as far as it went. Patterson said he knew nothing about the *Politician*.

'But you recorded for Miller,' I demurred, having heard this from Angus John.

'Yes,' he said, 'but what I told him was all second-hand. I don't know anything really.'

Neil Campbell said the same thing, but not quite so politely. 'I was away at the time in the merchant navy,' he added. I couldn't dispute this, so I asked him if he could get me over to Eriskay in his boat.

'I don't know about that,' he said. 'You'd best see John McIsaac'

'Where do I find him?'

'He'll be at Ludag with his boat tomorrow morning, 9.15.'

'And you think he'll take me?'

'Yes – he's got the mail-boat. He has to go.'

I rang off, thanked Jean the red-head, and went back to the bar. But closing time came at nine o'clock and I soon found myself banished to my room. I was depressed. Not a foot of tape had been recorded, and apart from my notes of the talk with Peter MacInnes I had nothing to show. Getting into my pyjamas, I fell to wondering if Angus John would keep putting me off, night by night. 'Actualities', as we call them in television, are notoriously scared of tape-recorders, even if they have nothing to hide.

Earlier in the evening, when we were in the bar, someone had pointed to the postman and said: 'Go and talk to him – he'll give you lots of stories about the *Polly*.' I went over as suggested, but at the mention of the word *Polly* a look of consternation and fear came over his face. He gulped down his beer and shot out through the door. This incident, followed by the refusal of the two men on the telephone, could only mean one thing; that the islanders – or most of them – still wished to keep their secrets. The job would obviously be harder than I had bargained for.

CHAPTER 3

The Quest Continues

IT IS VERY UNWISE, so I have discovered, to read a travel book about a place when you happen to be there yourself. The ideal plan is to absorb a few salient facts beforehand, and then read up the details afterwards. While you are actually on your journey, put the book away. The reason for this is that impressions conveyed by the printed word can never identify themselves with the more subjective impressions of the naked eye. It is like trying to mix recorded music with live music, the result being discord. I remember once reading a book about the Taj Mahal when I visited that famous monument, and coming to the conclusion that the author was an idiot. He talked of light and form and miracles of grace; but all I was conscious of was the heat, the flies, and the vulgar caterwauling of the guides who considered, quite wrongly, that they had not received adequate baksheesh.

Before going to the Outer Hebrides, therefore, I was determined to do my reading well in advance; but no sooner had the air tickets arrived than George More O'Ferrall, the head of drama at Anglia Television, rang up asking me to write some film sequences out of a play he had commissioned; thus my reading was postponed. Unfortunately, I am not one of those people who can read seriously in aeroplanes, and it was not until this first night in the hotel that I opened the books at all. Through various sources I had mustered three: Gordon Seton's *The Immortal Isles*, Alasdair Alpin MacGregor's *The Western Isles*, and Louis MacNeice's *I Crossed the Minch*. Seton's book came out in 1926, and, as one might gather from the title, he is (or was) very pro-Hebridean. His main interest is in wild life and he can talk of 'the musical clamour of the wild geese and the mournful baying of the grey seals'. He can also rise to a purple passage such as this:

> How wonderful is a perfect day of midsummer in the Isles! The horizon seems limitless. There are no trees to shade the sun and the light is brilliant. At sunrise the sky north east burns with a soft rosy glow, and the pale moon hangs like a sickle above the Minch where countless puffins and shear-waters fish, and the tribe of the herring, king of fishes, plays. At noontide, sea and land seem to slumber in intense heat.

Seton liked the islanders too. He calls them 'an attractive race – full of simplicity, dignity and charm'.

By contrast, Alasdair Alpin MacGregor comes like a cold douche. To him, the islanders are lazy, lying, dishonest, dirty, and drunken. For example: 'Two characteristics of the people which the stranger to the Western Isles is swift to observe, certainly so far as the male population is concerned, are laziness and drunkenness.' Even the innocent ritual of the boat nights comes under his lash:

> When the news goes around that the lights have been sighted it is still customary for all the young people, and indeed for all the middle-aged and elderly, to set out for the pier in time to see her come alongside. It is deemed essential for purposes of gossip and local knowledge, that as many islanders as possible should know just who arrived on such and such a night, what the passengers were wearing, how they looked in their city finery, what news they had of ongoings among relatives and friends on the mainland . . . The meeting of the mail boat . . . is still the principal event of the day.

Elsewhere in the book MacGregor declares himself a teetotaller and vegetarian, which may mean that his view on life is somewhat specialized. Certainly as my stay on the island lengthened I found fewer and fewer points of contact with him. But his book does contain a vast amount of data on the islands, and where he sticks to facts he is much more lucid. Curiously enough, though his book came out in 1949, thirteen years before my own visit, his ghost still seemed just ahead of me – like Miller's. Time after time when I told people I was a writer they would round on me with 'I hope you're not another Alasdair Alpin!' Hastily I would assure them that debunking was no part of my mission; the land and life of the Hebrides interested me only so far as it was bound up with the story of the *Politician*. Fortunately they seemed to believe me. But the bitterness caused by MacGregor's onslaught will, I think, linger in the islands for a generation or more.

Louis MacNeice was a colleague of mine in the BBC and for years we were both working on radio features, he on the more literary kind and myself on the more dramatic. Altogether we must have spent hundreds of hours drinking in the same pubs and the same bar, and I had known him by sight since the late forties, but no one had ever introduced us and we had never spoken. This I had always regretted, having a great admiration for his work and sharing his passion for Rugby football. This book was about a journey he made consciously, as a Celt, to discover if he had any real affinity to the Celts of the Hebrides. To his sorrow, it soon became evident that his lack of Gaelic was an insuperable barrier, reducing him immediately to the status of a tourist. He observed, as I did even on the first day, that when the islanders speak Gaelic they are alive, the words dance off their lips. But once they switch to English, their voices and expressions become dull, almost lifeless. One delightful man I was to record later said to me: 'Oh, if I could only record in Gaelic – instead of trying to wrap my tongue round English!' Actually, the islanders speak English beautifully, with a clarity of phrase and diction and an absence of slang which might serve as a model to anyone. Nevertheless it is only in Gaelic that their speech has wit and gaiety.

MacNeice's book was a disappointment to me on the whole, being full of annoying tricks of the thirties such as imaginary characters and even imaginary conversations. But, like all poets, when he makes the effort he can put a glow, a luminosity, into his prose and stun you with sudden revelations.

They hadn't told me that the east end of the island was the most attractive, so I took the road northwards from the hotel which goes across the island (two miles in width) to Annabost. The air was full of peewits, the fields covered with yellow flag-irises, big daisies, little daisies, buttercups and dandelions. The sheep were very white after shearing. There was a chilly breeze from the north – but the sun shone continuously. As I crossed a rise I saw the Northern Sea in front of me, intensely blue across the sandhills.

Gradually, as I read, the main Hebridean story began to take shape in my mind. As with all new subjects, the salient facts were slow to reveal themselves, and it was some time before I could begin fitting the details into their correct slots. The ancient name, it appears, was Innis Cat or Innis Fada, the Long Island, obviously derived from the fact that, from a distance, that is how the Hebrides appear. According to geologists they are very old, their foundation rocks being Lewisian gneiss. Some geologists say that this is the oldest rock formation in Europe; others declare that it is the oldest in the world. The rocks were formed under water and (as the earth contracted) were forced upwards under pressure so great that they melted, and in some areas formed a black glassy rock known as 'flinty crush'. On some of the polished rocks there are even scratch marks made by the glaciers as they passed over them, aeons back in time.

If the geologists believe that the islands are as old as this I am not one to argue. Certainly, walking over some of the more barren stretches, one can imagine without difficulty a brontosaurus or a dinosaur rising out of the lochs with a foul stink of breath, and padding ponderously across the black rocks. More sophisticated animals look out of place here.

The first known date is 888, when King Harald of Norway added the islands to his domain. There were inhabitants on the island centuries before that, and relics of their underground houses can still be found. The standing stones of Callernish, so the archaeologists tell us, were old before Romulus and Remus launched into the unlikely project of founding Rome. But whereas there are no records of pre-Norse times, the Norseman have at least left their sagas. These great seamen not only conquered the islands but stayed on to colonize them, and at one time they commanded the seas down as far as Arran and Bute. Magnus Barefoot, King of Norway, struck a bargain with the King of Scotland that he (Magnus) could claim any territory on the west coast round which he could steer his galley. Desiring to include Kintyre, he sat tight while his men pulled the galley right over the Isthmus linking Kintyre and Knapdale. He may have played this trick several times, for the word 'tarbert' which has come down in several place-names means literally 'draw-boats'; that is, cuts constructed artificially to avoid going round by sea.

Two centuries after 1066 comes 1265 and in that year (or, as some people think, in 1263) King Haco's fleet was defeated at the battle of Largs; and the Norsemen slowly departed, leaving behind a string of attractive place names, their songs, customs and their rich sailors' blood. Even today, seven centuries later, it is not bred out and you can meet tall, broad-shouldered blond men who might have come straight across from Stavanger, or Bergen or Kristianssen, on the last plane. Fortunately the Celtic tongue remained; and centuries later the islands were to be dominated by six clans – the MacNeils in Barra, the MacDonalds in Uist and Benbecula, the MacLeods (the descendants of Somerled the Viking) in Harris, and the MacAuleys, the MacIvers and the MacNichols in Lewis. For century after dark century there was to be war, pillage, robbery and piracy. In Lewis the Seaforths came to power. The Fourth Earl (Kenneth Og) crossed to Ireland with James to take part in the Siege of Londonderry. Later on he crossed over to Scotland for the Jacobite rising but his luck deserted him and he had to surrender to the Government. His son, Black William, supported the Old Pretender in the '15, and was charged with treason and forfeited his estates. A Hanoverian garrison arrived to occupy Lewis. From the fifteenth century the clans in the southern isles had fought each other in campaigns and skirmishes, the motives of which are lost in the mists. In the six-teenth century the French, the Spaniards and the Dutch discovered the fish in the Minch and sent up their boats, but the clans gave them a rough time of it. In the seventeenth century James VI licensed a group of thugs called the Fife Adventurers to exploit Lewis, but after three attempts they fell before the implacable hostility of the islanders.

Farther south, the MacNeils of Barra and the MacDonalds (the Clanranald of South Uist) raided each other, or the main-land. Both employed pirate ships and tried to gain the mastery of the seas. In the end the MacNeils won, but not before they had incurred the displeasure of Her Majesty Queen Elizabeth I of

England. Early in the seventeenth century the Crown tried to bring the islands into line and to stop them seizing boats and nets, but the chiefs resisted, especially the Clanranald who was intent on remaining master of his ancient territory. Finally the clans were forced by the Privy Council to enter into a bond requiring them to behave; but the Clanranald soon broke it and Roderick MacLeod was asked to bring him to heel. As Clanranald was his son-in-law and a fellow pirate, he was understandably reluctant. Soon the piracy (by the MacLeods, the MacNeils and the MacDonalds) became so rife that in 1622 the Privy Council laid down that no more ships should take wine and spirits to the island. Illicit stills became as thick as blackberries and it was some centuries before they all went out of business.

Barra and South Uist both took part in the march of the '45 in support of Bonny Prince Charlie. He had landed in Eriskay to launch his campaign; and after the disastrous defeat at Culloden he hid in a cave on South Uist. The Government offered £30,000 for information but no one betrayed him. Later, he was able to slip away to France.

On South Uist, the Clanranald lived in state, the chief even employing a 'piper bard' to sing the praises of his ancient house. The bards did not disappear until 1726, the last being Neil MacVurich, whose family had held this office for fifteen generations. The last of the harpists, Murdoch MacDonald, gave up his office in 1734 – he worked for the MacLeans of Coll.

By the dawn of the nineteenth century the great, wild days were over; even in the isles, piracy and plunder could no longer be looked on as a normal way of life. The clans had exhausted themselves. In 1834 the MacLeans of Harris sold up to the Earl of Dunmore for £60,000. A generation later Dunmore sold North Harris to the Scots. In 1888, John MacNeil, last of the MacNeils of Barra, sold his estate to Colonel John Gordon of

Cluny. In 1856 Lord MacDonald sold North Uist to Sir John Orde; and well before the nineteenth century was over not one of the Western Isles was owned by the old Hebridean families. From her first husband (John Gordon) Lady Gordon Cathcart inherited Barra, South Uist, Eriskay and Benbecula, but when she died in 1935 she had already sold the Barra estate (including Vatersay and the north end of Barra, which had already been disposed of to the Ministry of Agriculture) to Robert MacNeil, chief of the MacNeils of Barra. He at least owned eight thousand acres of the land of his forefathers, but did not choose to live on them; he had already made his home in New York. In 1944 Lady Gordon Cathcart's trustees sold the residue of the estate (less part of Barra which the Air Ministry had purchased) to Herman Anton Andreae, a London banker. It has since passed to a syndicate headed by Colonel Greig.

There is probably no nation in the world to which the past is such a living entity of daily life as the Scots. And in the isles (or so it seemed to me) the struggles, battles, failures, and rare successes of their ancestors whether Iberian, Viking or Scottish were a part of their very being. Even folk-lore lives on here, and great events are still celebrated by Gaelic songs. To judge, or even assess, these people by the standards and *mores* of South Kensington or Guildford – as some people have tried to do – seems to me quite purposeless.

The trouble is (and I do not claim to be completely guiltless myself) that we all have a tendency to become romantic about islands. We expect to find on them a beauty and simplicity of life that we have failed to find in our own country. And when in time we come to realize that the scenery, the life, and the people are very much the same as anywhere else, our disappointment turns unconsciously to resentment. We condemn the islanders for being no better than we are ourselves, for having no unusual virtues, and sharing our common vices. I have had quite a long experience of islands, and have lived on what must be one of the most delightful on earth, Ramree, off the coast of Burma. Therefore, forewarned, I went to the Hebrides determined not to make useless comparisons nor condemn, but to try and understand. As I realized only too well, unless I succeeded in gaining the sympathy of the islanders – and I had not made a very promising start – they would not talk to me and give me their stories. And if that happened, the facts about the *Politician* might vanish without trace.

On Saturday morning early I went to the garage and boarded a truck going to Ludag to meet the mail-boat. (This was just luck – I had no idea it was going till the *garagiste* told me.) Ludag is a point on the coast facing Eriskay, the channel being about a mile wide, and as we drove along the narrow road towards it the sun was still shining as it had done on Friday, with barely a cloud in the sky. The road ended at a sort of jetty, but a hundred yards or so back from this there were a couple of houses, and by one of them a large man in a beret was energetically digging a 'lazy bed' for planting potatoes. This, Allan said, was Neil Campbell; so I went over to have a talk with him. But he could not be bothered with me now, any more than on the telephone the previous night; and when I suggested that in the event of John McIsaac not being able to take me across to Eriskay on Monday he might possibly help, he snapped back, 'No – I shall be over in Barra.' Not wishing to continue a conversation with someone who obviously found my presence so disagreeable, I turned my back and walked down to the jetty. Here precisely at 9.15 am a boat came chugging across the placid waters, rounded the jetty wall, and came to anchor just a few yards away from me.

John McIsaac was a small man, very intelligent and courte-ous, and as soon as his passengers had clambered out of the boat I told him what I wanted. In reply he explained that he could not take me across now but would be very glad to do so at 12.15 on Monday. Also he promised to get together a few of the people on Eriskay most likely to have stories for me. We shook hands and he jumped back into the boat. I stood watching him sail away towards the blue hills of Eriskay.

At three o'clock I had a further disappointment. As Mrs McColl let me into her house, she eyed the tape-recorder very much as if it were a time-bomb, remarking curtly: 'There'll be no using that this afternoon.' At first I thought it was some personal antipathy towards this new-fangled gadget, but she added: 'I thought I'd never hear the word *Politician* again. . . it killed my husband.'

But now we were seated on either side of her comfortable lounge. An old campaigner at this game, I explained politely that if she did not wish to talk, I had no desire to press her. . . that the last thing I wished to do was intrude into her personal affairs. This broke the ice, and as she talked on, explaining why she did not wish to talk, she let drop several useful facts. They were mostly unconnected and would need checking, but anyway they were something to be going on with. Leaving her house, after tea and scones, I passed an attractive woman in her thirties who was tending her garden. Stopping to congratulate her I said that this was the first real garden I had seen on the islands. Thanking me, she explained that she came from the Lake District, and what she missed most of all was the sight of daffodils in the spring. Hence her efforts to grow them here, together with tulips and a variety of rock plants. I asked her why the islanders did not bother to cultivate their gardens.

'Because there is no tradition of gardening here,' she explained. 'You can understand why. The wind is so strong that after a gale when you go out into the garden it looks as if there has been a fire – all the plants are black. We call it 'the blast'.'

I asked why they did not build walls. 'The wind changes with the seasons,' she said, 'and you'd need walls all the way round. People have tried building squares, but what happens is the wind gets inside and spins round like a top – and then everything is wiped out.'

I went to the garage to find that the car I had ordered was not in yet, so I arranged to hire it the next day, Sunday, instead. Meanwhile, there was nothing to do but take some photographs, record some notes on my talk with Mrs McColl, and – smartly at five o'clock – to join Wilson and Colonel Cameron in the cocktail bar. We kept off military history this time, and talked of the Colonel's seaweed factory near Kilpheder. He explained that the islanders cut the rock-weed all the year round, and gathered the tangle in the winter months. About 150 men did the job of collecting, and they could earn about £12 a week. Apart from them, he had about forty men in his factory here, and some more in a factory up at North Uist. I asked him what he did with the seaweed and he explained that chemicals called 'algenates' were extracted which had a thousand uses in industry. They were even used as suspension agents in orangeade.

We were interrupted by the hotel porter, a wild-eyed man with delusions of glory, who insisted on buying us drinks. He boasted that Frank Owen was a great friend of his.

'He opened my club for me in London,' he said. I wondered to myself why, if he had a club in London, he was cleaning the boots in Lochboisdale, and tested him out with a few questions about Frank Owen. But he knew all the answers, even which building and which floor Owen had his office in. He went on to try and inveigle the Colonel and Wilson into arguments about the respective merits of various Scottish regiments, but they weren't having any. So finally he downed his drink saying, 'It's my regimental dinner tonight, and I'm stuck here.' Then, to our relief, he marched out.

At seven o'clock promptly I was back in the public bar to round up Angus John. He was much more relaxed this evening, and after a couple of pints turned to me and said, 'Shall we go up and record?'

I led him round to the front of the hotel and upstairs to my room. He took an almost professional interest in the recorder, comparing it with other models he had seen, and was surprisingly knowledgeable. I switched on and we talked for about an hour and a half. To my surprise he told me that years before the accident he had served aboard the *Politician* as an able seaman, adding with a chuckle, 'This came in useful, you see – when we went to find the whisky I knew my way about it.'

He told me all he knew of the story, speaking fluently, colourfully, and patiently making a point clear if I failed to grasp it. Occasionally he would break off from his narrative to explain his attitude to the Customs or the police, or his views on the law. He was not very good on dates but he was excellent when it came to significant details, and anecdotes. On some things he was decidedly prejudiced, but frank enough to admit it. He said that he had been born on South Uist and would die there but (like so many of the islanders) he had travelled widely and knew Panama, Vancouver, New York, Sydney, Bombay, Singapore, Hong Kong, and in fact all the great ports of the world. He said that he was 66 and 'just about retired'. He didn't think he had much longer to live, for, as he put it, 'I don't feel so strong the noo.' Then catching my look of surprise, he rocked with laughter. 'I think that's enough,' he said. 'Let's get back to the beer, shall we?'

There was just time for one more drink before they closed.

Although this was Saturday night and the Hebrideans are supposed to be heavy drinkers, I only saw one man the worse for wear. A good many people, however, were buying half bottles of whisky to take home – no doubt to keep them going through Sunday when the pubs would be closed all day.

I knew there was no use trying to see anyone on Sunday. In Scotland the natives cease to live on this day and are content to merely exist in a state of half-frozen suspension. But I had the car for the day, an old Austin, and in the morning I drove out to the west coast to try and find the seals. Since reading Gordon Seton's book I had acquired a strong desire to crawl up and photograph them and to hear 'their mournful baying', as he called it. But I was out of luck. Either they were not there or I could not find them. When driving along, however, one thing that impressed me was the state of the crofts. Time and again I would see the old building half derelict or used as a barn, while next door to it would be a modern house or bungalow, and every croft seemed to have a brand new tractor, apart from a car. This betokened a standard of living quite different from that depicted in any accounts of the island, and I fell to wondering how the change had come about. Why, if they were as lazy and drunken as MacGregor and others had said they were, should the crofters have bothered to acquire such equipment? Some months later I was to read an article in *The Times* by Sir Robert Urquhart, Chairman of the Crofters Commission, who said that to the surprise of everyone a strong movement had come from the crofters themselves and now, with the aid of grants from the Commission, great strides were being made to improve the standard of husbandry.

After a lunch I took Jean the red-head and we went out to the coast by Orosay, a small islet connected to South Uist by a rocky causeway. The sun was still shining, the wind had dropped, and the day was warm. Scrambling to the top of the hill which I suppose was a hundred feet or more above the sea, we could marvel at the white Hebridean sand stretching on either side of us, between the blue Atlantic and the green machar. In the distance lay the mountains, no longer dun as I had first seen them, but a dark, almost royal, blue. The air was strong and even the silence (which on the first day I had found almost hostile) had a magic quality about it. The sheep were wandering over the islet, cropping the tough grass, but here and there we could see the pathetic sight of a dead lamb. I thought at first they must have fallen to their deaths on the rocks, but then noticed that each one had its eyes pecked out by a black-backed gull. It was, I think, on this Sunday afternoon that the absence of trees no longer bothered me and I could appreciate for the first time the strange beauty of these islands, and understand the fierce attachment of the Hebrideans – their desire to live in their own way, unfettered by restrictions from London or Edinburgh. Viewed from Orosay, these great cities seemed infinitely distant and improbable, the only realities being sky and sea, and sand and mountain. Perhaps, I thought, it was this feeling which explained why so many rulers, from Queen Elizabeth onwards, had failed to make the islanders toe the line. It might also, I suspected, go some way to explaining their attitude towards the *Politician*.

At 11.30 on Monday Allan drove me over to Ludag. My luck still held and the weather was perfect, the islands standing out clear and shining across the Sound. I left my tape-recorder in a shed by the concrete wall and walked back to find the house of John MacKinnon who, the Colonel had mentioned, might be useful to me. He was not there, but a boy led me across the fields to a peat cut where MacKinnon and two young men were working. The peat went down to a depth of nearly eight feet and already they had cut several hundred bricks which were lying in the sun to dry. No one spoke, so I waited till MacKinnon had finished a complete spit before moving up to him. He was a lean, sharp-witted man with a rather quizzical air about him.

'Good morning,' I said. 'Mr John MacKinnon?'

'I am very probably.'

'My name is Swinson. I'm looking for material on the *Politician*. Could you help me?'

'I might do.'

'Well, I don't want to worry you while you're busy. Could I come and talk this evening?'

'I dare say you could.'

'Would six o'clock be all right?'

'It very probably would.' Then, after a pause: 'If you bring a bottle.'

Promising this should be done, I walked back to the road, then turned left for Ludag. A rabbity little man was seated on the grass by the jetty, and as he eyed me suspiciously I asked him if he also were waiting for John McIsaac.

'That's right,' he said grudgingly, as if parting with a great secret.

'He said he'd be here by noon – but I can't see him coming.'

'He'll be here. Are you going to Eriskay?'

'Yes – I'm searching for stories about the *Politician*.'

'*Politician*!' He froze immediately. 'They won't talk to you on Eriskay.'

'John McIsaac thought they might.'

'No – no, they won't!' He turned away from me, so I left him and walked along to a grassy bank. Here I lay down and was soon asleep in the sun, to be woken a quarter of an hour later by the sound of the boat chugging towards me on the calm water.

Scrambling to my feet and picking up the tape recorder, I walked along the top of the concrete wall, moving carefully to avoid slipping on the wet seaweed. By now the boat had rounded the wall, a rope had been thrown and caught, and John McIsaac was leaping ashore. Waiting till his passengers had landed and made their way past me to the road, he came up close and said,

'I've had a talk with the people, but they won't see you.'

This was a blow. 'None of them?' I asked, but he shook his head.

'I saw Neil Gillies, the only one left of the men who went to prison. But he told me he'd served his sentence and he didn't want to talk about it.'

This was the first time I had heard that men were sent to prison, so immediately I began asking for details – how many of them, and for how long?

'There were three from Eriskay,' he said, 'and two of them are dead. What happened on the other islands I can't tell you.'

I asked about the wreck. 'Could you take me out to Calvay and show me the site of the accident?'

'Aye, I could do that.'

With an 'I told you so' look on his face, the rabbity little man jumped into the boat and we pushed off. The waters were shallow, and here and there I could see rocks beneath the surface of the clear water. As McIsaac steered round them carefully I talked to him about the *Politician*. Though he knew nothing personally, he told me that the boat we were in (the *St Joseph*) belonged to his father, and was the boat that McColl had hired to chase the looters. This was a useful piece of information, tying up with the Customs reports.

Calvay lies at the eastern end of the sound, that is at the entrance to the Minch, and we went round to the far side of it so that I could photograph the site of the accident. This took only a few moments, and I looked around to marvel at the extraordinary position into which the ship had got herself. Then McIsaac took me a few hundred yards towards the coast of South Uist and pointed to a black shape on the bottom, under about two fathoms of water.

'There she is,' he said.

'What?'

'The *Politician*'

'All of it?'

'No – the rear half. They cut her in two, you know. This is the No. 5 hold – where the whisky is.'

Peering down into the shallow water, a hundred questions were already buzzing around in my brain, questions I should somehow have to investigate before I left the islands. Why was she cut in half? Why did they leave the half with the whisky in? Who were 'they'? What had happened to the other half? And so on. . .

Back on land at Ludag, I sat and finished my sandwiches, then took the tape-recorder to John MacKinnon's house. Luckily there was a suitable plug point, so leaving it in the custody of his wife and daughter, till six in the evening, I set out to walk the six miles to Daliburgh.

My object there was to visit a Mrs Mitchell who, according to Miss Shand of the Highland Industries, was the widow of the Ministry of Agriculture official, and knew all about the *Politician*. (I should have mentioned earlier that Miss Shand had kindly given me a '*Polly* bottle' – empty, but at least a tangible link with the story I was investigating.) The long walk was necessary as the car had gone back to Lochboisdale and there was no other means of transport. But it did not matter, for though the day was hot I was in no hurry, and there was the pleasant feeling at the back of my head that the exercise might rid me of a few surplus pounds. For an hour or more things went well, but then my right foot began protesting that it had not been used to such treatment for some years, and I was quite relieved to see a bus parked by a farm. To my disappointment, however, a woman standing near by told me that it would not be leaving for a couple of hours or more; so I kept on walking. Farther on, near Pollachar, I heard a growling in the ditch by the roadside and walked over to investigate. A black sheepdog was tearing the guts out of a dead sheep and didn't want any interference. I turned right along the straight road for Daliburgh and had gone two miles or more before anything overtook me. Then there came a small van, driven at breakneck speed by a youth with a cigarette dangling from his lips. I signalled for a lift but he ignored me and roared on. I hurled every epithet I could think of after him and continued walking till the roofs of Daliburgh were in sight over the rocky plain. Half an hour later they had not come appreciably nearer but, to my surprise, a car came up from behind me and stopped. In it was a Mr D G S MacNeil, the licensee of the Pollachar Inn which, as I knew, by legend was the inn where Bonny Prince Charlie had his first dram on Scottish soil, on his way to the mainland and the march of the '45. MacNeil told me that he was having great trouble over water and couldn't develop his business till pipes were carried to the inn.

'I've told the council,' he said. 'But they just talk and do nothing about it. I'm having to search the place for old wells but I can't keep carting water all the time.' (A few weeks later MacNeil was to feature in a column in *The Stage* for refusing the BBC permission to film his inn for a thriller serial. 'Why should we feature in entertainment for television on the mainland,' he said to the reporter, 'when the BBC hold out no hope for building a station for us?')

Just in time for a delightful Scottish tea, I arrived at Mrs

Mitchell's house in Daliburgh. A charming, cultured old lady, she drew back in mock horror at the mention of the word *Politician*.

'It's caused so much trouble in these islands,' she said, 'and I'm not sure it's safe to speak about it even yet.'

'What sort of trouble?' I asked.

'Well. . . bitterness.'

'Who is bitter, and why?'

She shook her head. 'We keep our secrets in the islands,' she said.

In an attempt to extract some of these secrets, I asked her about the men who were arrested and sent to prison, but she was reluctant to talk. Neither did she explain what she meant by bitterness, or enlighten me as to who was bitter about what.

I got a lift back to Lochboisdale in a greengrocery van, along with a mother, her baby, and about a thousand packets of detergent.

At six o'clock I hired a car from the garage and drove back to West Kilbride in high hopes of obtaining a long and profitable recording from John MacKinnon. The daughter let me in but there was a strained silence.

'He's not here,' she said. 'He's had to go away in his boat.'

'How long for?'

'About a week, I should think.'

'A week?' I was rather annoyed and could not help showing it. 'Didn't he know about this when I spoke to him this morning?' She gave a weak smile.

'No – he's got three fishing-boats, you see. . . and one of them had a man short. I'm sorry.'

The story smelt but there was no use arguing, so I got back into the car and drove to Lochboisdale. I was very depressed. The next day I was due to leave South Uist to travel up to Lochmaddy; and the only people who had really talked to me were Peter MacInnes and Angus John. Their material was good but still left large gaps, and there were a hundred details that needed checking. Also I was oppressed by the feeling that there was a lot more to know – and once I'd left South Uist it would escape me for ever.

Back at the hotel I went into the dining-room for high tea. Wilson was not there, the new manager having asked him to find accommodation elsewhere, but Jean the red-head was just finishing her meal. She told me about the two strange maids whom I had seen wandering desolately about the hotel.

'They're Spanish,' she said, 'and came over here to learn English. The agent told them they would be working in London. As it is they're stuck up here, and hear nothing but Gaelic. They say they want to die.'

Jean went back on duty and the Colonel came in. We talked of Alasdair Alpin MacGregor's book and the remarks in his chapter on the algenate industries. The Colonel was very bitter about them, but in my own despondent mood the feud between MacGregor and the islanders seemed remote and unimportant. All I could think of was that the story of the *Politician* was slipping out of my grasp. The Colonel finished his meal, rolled his napkin and was just about to get up and leave the room when he said, 'By the way, my manager, Norman MacMillan, has some stories for you. He lives at Kilpheder. First bungalow on the right. He'll be back about nine o'clock.'

Slightly more cheerful, I went around to the public bar to have a farewell drink with Angus John. He was in his usual corner and greeted me like an old friend. While we sank our beer I suddenly remembered a name which had been mentioned by a man at the hotel the previous day – Donald Curry.

'Donald Curry!' Angus repeated with surprise. 'That's him over there.'

Curry was a large, powerful man with a strong Viking strain in him, and at Angus's bidding he came over to us. But he didn't know anything about the *Politician* himself, he said. His brother John was the one. Expecting to receive an answer that John was abroad or at sea, I asked whether I could find him. But – 'He's just outside,' said Donald. 'I'll get him.'

Ten minutes later, John Curry and Angus John were both in my room, drinking whisky and recording stories of the *Polly*. John was younger than his brother, but just as large and blond and, unlike Angus, he had a cold, factual view of things. This gave me a chance to check some of Angus's stories, and for Angus himself to defend or modify them, as he thought fit. After an hour Curry became restless, glanced at his watch, and said he ought to be going. So we all said goodbye, Curry driving back to his croft, Angus returning to his corner in the bar, and myself driving to Kilpheder to keep my appointment with Norman MacMillan.

When I arrived, the house was dark, but as cars were still coming back from the boat – it was another boat night – I thought that his would be among them, so I sat and waited. The head-lights of the cars as they drove along the main road, then swung round towards me, became less frequent and after half an hour they ceased altogether. Everything became dark and quiet and I began wondering if I had got the wrong house; but fortunately a young man came walking along with his dog and I was able to check with him. 'Yes,' he said, 'that's Norman's house all right. But he's not there now.' Resisting the temptation to reply that his absence was the cause of my asking, I sat down again. By ten o'clock I was wondering if the Colonel had got things wrong. . . by ten-fifteen I had reached the pitch of asking myself why I had come to the Hebrides anyway. Was I on a wild-goose chase? Should I cut my losses and get back to the relative sanity of the television studios? But before I had time to pursue these morbidities too far, an estate car seemed to come out of nowhere, and out got MacMillan and his wife and daughters. Introductions were difficult in the dark, so we went inside, and I could see that he was a large, rather distinguished-looking man, in his late forties or early fifties. His elder daughter was depressed, having failed her driving test that afternoon, so we spent a few moments commiserating with her and discussing some of the trickier points of the Highway Code. Then she and her younger sister withdrew, MacMillan found me a suitable plug point, and, watched by his wife, we got down to business.

Like most of the islanders, he spoke clearly and fluently, but without a great deal of expression. After a few minutes he said to me: 'Oh, if only we could talk in Gaelic – it's such a business wrapping my tongue round English!' But it did not matter at all. We had not been going long before I realized with a great surge of excitement that this was the man I had been looking for. His memory was good, his eye for detail was sharp, and he had a wealth of anecdote. I only had to prompt him, or suggest some new line of conversation for a whole spate of stories to come forth. But all the time there was the feeling that he was not exaggerating or striving after effect. If I stopped him to query a point, the explanation was available and never had to be groped for. I suppose that an hour and a half had gone by before I mentioned 'The Song of the *Politician*' – a Gaelic ballad that I had often heard rumours of, but never managed to trace. I had long come to the conclusion, in fact, that it must have been an ephemeral song of the moment and long forgotten; perhaps it was even just a few words put to an old tune. But MacMillan knew what I meant at once. 'Good God,' he said, 'I'll sing it to you, if you like!'

I heard later on that he was a well-known singer in the

islands and a frequent performer at ceilidhs, but immediately I could sense that his voice had an unusual quality. There was a fire and richness about it, a barbaric quality which proclaimed that the *Politician* was as secure in legend and song as Magnus Barefoot or Somerled.

Towards one o'clock I switched off the recorder with a sense of relief and satisfaction. I could now tell the story of the islanders' attack on the *Politician*; and of the authorities' attack on the islanders. As I drove down the dark road towards Lochboisdale the main shape of it was already forming in my mind.

CHAPTER 4

The Islanders Attack

ON THE MORNING of 6 February 1941, Captain Worthington and his officers, together with the Bosun and the carpenter, were taken back to the *Politician* by the lifeboat which had rescued them the previous evening. Their object was to see if there was any hope of refloating her, but even a short inspection was enough to convince them that any such idea was out of the question. To make matters worse, the gales were still continuing and there was a strong likelihood that she would start to break up. The officers, to their surprise, found that there had been visitors on board during the night who had gone through the cabins, filching personal possessions; to his annoyance, Huntington found that his radio had been taken.

The only record of the Captain's demeanour at this time is that 'he was most upset'. Anyone asking him how the accident had happened was met with a silent glare, or at best with a shrug or a look of bewilderment. Like Swain, and indeed all the officers, he was quite mystified; and now, with the knowledge that for all practical purposes his ship was doomed, his thoughts must have been sombre, to say the least. After commanding ships and sailing all the oceans and seas of the world for forty years or more, he had come to grief less than twenty-four hours after leaving his home port. He would have to leave this fine ship, cargo and all, to the mercy of the rocks and savage seas of these remote islands. The whole experience must have seemed unreal, like an ugly dream after a feverish night.

Though he did not know it, news of the disaster had spread

all over England – thanks to William Joyce, alias Lord Haw-haw, who announced in his early morning bulletin that the *Politician* 'was lost with all hands'. Fortunately the telegrams from the crew, dispatched from Barra, had already reached their wives and families before the broadcast, so they were left in no doubt. But many people, lacking any other source of information, believed the German version, and very often, even today, it is asserted that there were no survivors.

Donald Ferguson, the Lloyd's agent (who had a shop in Lochboisdale) now succeeded in reaching the ship, and, after a short conversation with Worthington he signalled to London:

> Steamer *Politician* lies on flat rock in Eriskay Sound. Water in engine-room. Draught 23 feet at stern; 21 feet at bows. 2,000 tons of valuable cargo. Light draught steamer could dock alongside. Needs pumps. Could superintend operations from Eriskay quite close.

The Radio Officer was able to signal:

> 11 am. Part of crew aboard. Vessel laying quiet. Five feet of water in hold; 23 feet in engine-room; 11 feet in No. 5 hold. Still awaiting assistance. Intend leaving vessel at dusk and returning at daylight.

The movements of the officers were not unobserved. Keen eyes were following them from the hills of Eriskay and South Uist. Fishermen passing up or down the Sound had time to linger and manoeuvre round them. As Norman MacMillan said to me: 'We were very interested in that boat all the time. We asked kindly after her every day and got first-hand information.'

Another visitor to the ship was Charles McColl, the Customs

Officer stationed at Lochboisdale. He had telephoned his superior at Portree on Skye, Ivan Gledhill, immediately he heard the news, and on the morning of the 6th he had rung Archie McIsaac asking him to take him out in the *St Joseph*. Captain Worthington was not glad to see him; in fact both he and Swain refused to make any deposition or to state the nature of the cargo. Whether McColl already knew that there was whisky aboard it is impossible to say, but in any case it is unlikely that he had any idea of the quantity. Worthington's and Swain's attitude is, of course, quite understandable. They were expecting to face an inquiry and the less they said to Government officials the better. But the fact remains that if they had co-operated with McColl from these early days, a good deal of trouble might have been saved for everyone concerned.

On the 7th and 8th the officers again went to the ship in the morning and returned to Barra at dusk, but there was little they could do except to make ready important items of cargo, for the time when the coaster arrived from the Liverpool and Glasgow Salvage Association, and take the breach-block off the 4.7 gun on the stern. On the 9th, the coaster *Ranger* came alongside. Huntington managed to connect a steam-pipe on it to a pipe aboard the *Politician*, raising enough power to get the winches in action, and in two days some five hundred tons of cargo were transferred – mostly cars, bicycles and cotton goods. The Skipper of the *Ranger* sent off a signal giving his own estimate of the *Politician*'s condition:

All double-bottomed tanks pierced. No. 1 hold leaking slightly. No. 2 hold dry. Machinery space and No. 6 hold full and tidal. No. 5 hold full. Soundings show vessel supported from boilers aft and unsupported for'd of boilers but water-borne. As vessel lies end on to bad weather, salvage considered practicable but speculative and will require a large assemblage of pumping power. Will make pumping test as soon as possible.

But on the 11th the gales returned and the salvors were unable to board her; in fact the *Ranger* even failed to get alongside. The position did not improve on the 12th and 13th; the wind had now backed from south to east but was still as strong. On the 14th the *Ranger* had to make the journey to Stornaway, a hundred miles to the north, to take on more fuel, but when she returned the following morning the weather had fortunately moderated. Commander Kay, the Salvage Officer, was now in charge and sent divers down to examine the ship's bottom. They reported that the ship had suffered considerably during the last few days; the stern frame was broken and the rudder post bent to an angle of 45 degrees. Sixty feet of keel were shattered and there was a fracture near the main injection fourteen feet long and twelve inches wide. All compartments aft of No. 2 hold were tidal and contained fuel oil.

Meanwhile the *Ranger* continued to take off cargo, notably two hundred and sixty bags of mail and several cases of what was listed mysteriously as 'special cargo'. (At first I thought this was a euphemism for banknotes, but I was wrong about this, as will be seen later.) It was about this time that Huntington asked Commander Kay why no attempt was being made to salvage the whisky. Kay replied: 'It's not worth the effort. Apart from the fact that it's not worth very much, the salt water will have got in anyway.'

The transfer of the cargo went on during the 18th and the 19th. Despite the report of the divers, Kay was by no means despondent. He signalled:

I consider that salvage of ship still possible and operations proceeding.

To help with the transfer of the cargo the salvors had recruited four local crofters, among them John Curry of South Uist. The news that there was whisky aboard had spread from Barra to Eriskay and from Eriskay to South Uist, and even though the work was hard and the money was only a few shillings, Curry (as he put it) 'was delighted to be aboard that ship'. Tentatively he made inquiries as to which hold the whisky might be in, to receive the reply: 'It's in No. 5 hold. All of it.' The hatch was still down and (as he knew) the hold was waterlogged and tidal. But the knowledge might still be useful – if the salvors left anything.

On the 20, more cargo was taken off and Commander Kay carried out pumping tests. As the fair weather held, the work went on smoothly till the 24th when the Commander came to an important decision. He signalled:

'Regret exhaustive pumping tests and divers' examination shows salvage of vessel impracticable.' In other words, the ship was doomed. Efforts to save the cargo were intensified, the steamer *Corteen* coming into action, and soon the salvors were able to report that:

> The bulk of sound cargo from between decks has been transferred to coaster which is now discharging in Glasgow. The balance of sound cargo, together with the valuable ships' materials, will be transferred to another coaster.

Though Kay did not apparently realize it, some of the salvage men had got down into No. 5 hold and acquired a very useful stock of whisky for themselves. Unfortunately, when the coaster arrived in Glasgow, a Customs rummage crew came aboard and found the whisky hidden in the fo'c'sle. However, the men learned by their mistake and on the next run they packed their precious load into a bag and hurled it over the side while the ship was in the Crinan Canal. They had made arrangements for someone to pick it up, and, having docked, they travelled back to reclaim it.

On the 27th, Worthington and his officers left Lochboisdale for Glasgow. For their work on the salvage operation they had each been paid the princely sum of 30s. a day. Worthington and Swain had somehow managed to avoid speaking to Charles McColl or indeed any other officials. The crew had already left.

On 8 March, Ivan Gledhill went out to the wreck with Charles McColl. Gledhill had already written to his colleagues in Liverpool asking them to forward the outward files of the *Politician*; and it was from them that he learned the size of the whisky cargo. He was very much concerned; for already during the night of 19 February looters had got aboard and cleared the ship's bonded stores – i.e. the stores for the use of the officers and crew during the voyage. Their haul had been relatively small – thirty pounds of tobacco, two bottles of whisky, two of brandy and four tins of tea – but the incident did illustrate the fact that although the salvors considered it unsafe to remain aboard the ship during the night, the islanders were quite willing to take the risk.

Gledhill took up with Kay the question of the whisky, but again Kay repeated his view that it was not worth worrying about. So he went with McColl to inspect the No. 5 hold, which was found flooded with water and fuel oil; but on the surface there were a few lumps visible, and those, so the salvors said, were cases of whisky. Gledhill did all he could; had the hold battened down and sealed with a Customs seal, but he was very uneasy. As he knew only too well, it was impossible to obtain watchmen, and even if they could be found their dependability would be doubtful, to say the least. He therefore wrote to his superiors in London asking for instructions. To achieve complete revenue security, he said, he would require enough officers to maintain a constant motorboat patrol. As expected, however, his superiors replied that the men were not available and he must do the best he could. What this meant in practice was that he gave McColl orders to take any action he might think necessary, and to keep him informed of developments.

On 12 March the salvors reported that the discharge of cargo had been completed as far as possible. As the signal put it:

> Salvage vessel *Ranger* with Liverpool and Glasgow Salvage Association officer, left for Belfast yesterday having abandoned steamer *Politician*.

'Having abandoned the steamer *Politician*. . .' This was the news the islanders had been waiting for. As Angus John put it: 'When the salvors quit a ship – she's ours!' And here was the *Politician* with twenty thousand cases of whisky in the hold – good Scotch whisky which, if left to the mercy of the sea, would never be tasted by man or woman. By some extraordinary process the news of the salvors' departure had travelled right across the island in a matter of hours, to reach as far south as Barra Head, as far north as Harris, and as far west as Skye and Mull. It had even travelled to the mainland. To the people of Eriskay, the *Politician* was 'our boat'; but soon to their annoyance they were to find that the other islanders had different ideas. It was not as if this were peacetime, with drink plentiful; on the contrary the war had been on now for eighteen months and all that the islanders could buy was a few drams. Certainly in Lochboisdale the hotelier, Finlay MacKenzie, had a good stock – the rumour ran that there were five bedrooms all crammed to the ceiling with cases, but there was no knowing if this was true. Also, with the Government in England always putting up the duty, the native drink of the Scots was getting too expensive. But here was whisky galore. . . and whisky free. Whisky that neither the owners nor the salvors seemed to have any use for. Whatever the effort, whatever the danger, they must get it.

The number of boats in the islands was very limited, most of them being only rowing-boats. In March the waters of the Sound of Eriskay and the Minch can be dangerous, especially at night, but from all over the islands parties were setting forth. Norman MacMillan remembers:

> There were six of us and we rowed all the way from Strome to Calvay. That would be a distance of about twelve miles and it took us nearly four hours. It was terrible going. The current changed at one point and we nearly got carried out to sea.

But after all this effort their hopes were to be disappointed. When they arrived at the *Politician* several other boats were already there, and the crews told them the tide was so high that they would never get into the hold. The water and oil was right up to the deck. But if they couldn't reach the whisky there were other things. MacMillan says:

> We discovered some stout cases, and while we were dealing with them a few other boats came along and they took the bottles out of the cases and put them into bags. Then they slung them over the side. Anything you got hold of was so slippery – there was oil all over the deck and soon over you. There was an old man in the boat, down at the receiving end, stowing the bottles as they came over the rail. I heard someone shout and a calico bag parted from the rope and came down like a shot. The old man jumped from the bow of the boat to the stern and he was not a second too early. That bag full of good stout smashed on

the bow of the boat and the place was all fume and froth. Oh! It was a great time altogether.'

While they were working (if that is the term for it) the wind had got up and the wreck was moaning and heaving. The only thing to do was to look on the trip as a reconnaissance and to start rowing back.

The plan was to sail round to Lochboisdale – that is, round the south east corner of South Uist, and up the Minch – so they hoisted their 'rag of a sail' and set forth. But once they were exposed to the wind in the Minch 'the sail split right up to the yard' and the only hope was to turn about and head west up the Sound for Ludag. The water was coming in over the bows and they had to keep baling, hour after hour. But in the end they got there.

It was now obvious to MacMillan and his party, as it was to Angus John and others, that it would be impossible to get down to the bottom of the hold, even at low water. No one could swim in the filth and oil. The tactics would be to get on to the lower deck, half-way down the hold, then hook the cases up. This posed the problem as to what tool to use, as boat-hooks were too thick to pass under the wire. It was a problem that was soon solved. Men got to work in their crofts and hammered out hooks with a sharp point, something like Beefeaters' halberds, which they called 'spears'. The idea was that the point would pass easily through the wire, levering it out from the side of the case so that the hook could then catch under it. At least, that was the theory; only experience could tell if it worked.

The following night and for many nights to come, towards low tide boats approached the *Politician* from all directions – from South Uist, from Eriskay, from Barra, from North Uist, and some it is said from as far away as Lewis and Mull. The crews had equipped themselves with Tilly lamps and ropes and they manoeuvred themselves alongside the *Politician*. There was only one way of boarding her, by a rope ladder which hung from the deck, some fifty feet down to the water. Owing to the list of the ship it was well away from the side, difficult to climb up and even harder to climb down. Men – especially the more elderly – would swing to and fro in mid-air as their feet fumbled for the rungs. Beneath them the men waiting their turn in the boats would shout encouragement or curses, according to whether the climber happened to belong to their own boat or another. If the water was choppy – as it usually was – the boats would be jostling and bumping, one against the other. On the deck and in the hold, men – sometimes twenty or thirty of them, some nights even as many as fifty – would be moving around with their Tilly lamps and spears, their faces, hands and clothing black with oil. Sometimes they would recognize old friends or relatives they had not seen for years, and break off for a moment to catch up on the news. Most men brought some old clothes with them to save their best (or better) clothes. But even these became so clogged with oil that, after a few visits, some of them had to raid their wives' wardrobes, carrying off dresses, overalls, and even skirts to put over them. The *Politician* at night, with these black-faced, strangely garbed creatures, must have presented a strange sight indeed. Considering that man after man on the islands has the same or a similar name, it is a wonder that the teams did not get inextricably mixed up, muddle each other's winnings, and start arguing or fighting. But somehow, even in the darkness, the filth, the wet, not to mention the fumes and acrid stink of the fuel oil, they seemed to work happily together. No one can remember any arguments.

Naturally, even with the most highly organized team, things could go wrong – with the hazards confronting them, it was to be expected. To begin with, the whisky was not on the top of the cargo. As Norman MacMillan explained: 'It was covered with bundles of all sorts of clothing and everything you can think of – buckets to bicycles.' The clothing was large rolls of coloured cottons, destined for Jamaica, and to begin with, tons of it had to be hooked up and brought on deck. There were also countless thousands of shirts which, when washed and laundered, were quite presentable and lasted the islands for years. The whisky was stacked round the sides of the hold, not conveniently in the centre, so the men had to probe around with their long 'spears' (which had turned out to be a great success) until they touched something hard which felt like a case. The next job was to feel round the sides of it carefully for the wire, then slip the 'spear' underneath. A good pull, and if they were lucky the case would come clean out of the black water. When this happened there would be shouts of jubilation – just as, if the case were caught in coils of a roll of cloth and escaped off the hook, there would be curses and shrieks of disappointment. Getting the cases to the upper deck and on to the unloading point was no easy matter either. As already mentioned, the deck was slippery with its thick coating of oil, and it sloped down with the list of the ship. With only Tilly lamps to guide them, the men would slip and go sprawling, till they eventually reached their own pile of cases, which then had to be slung over the side. Sometimes they would be lowered into the wrong boat and there would be frantic warnings and shouting from deck to boat and from boat to deck. And sometimes the boatman, tired of waiting, would decide to sample the contents of cases already loaded, rendering operations more difficult than ever.

But to return to the hold. Norman MacMillan gave me this description:

It would be about a hundred feet long or more – and about half as much across. The men would be as thick as flies in it – moving around with Tilly lamps like so many glowworms in the dark. There'd be one expert on the cross beams, probing for the whisky and bringing it to the surface. The other two would be dragging it up, taking it over the deck and stacking it in heaps. You'd see fifty or sixty boxes right round the hold. When the tide turned there was another job of slinging it on the deck. The way we used to do that – a rope was no use – was to unroll some bales of calico. There was loads of it, beautiful shirting about forty yards long. You just got the loose end and let it unroll. When you got to the other end you tied it round the case and pulled it up on to the top deck. Well, once you got it there, you were safe enough from the tide. . . and you slung the case over the side into the boat.

The tide in the Sound of Eriskay can rise as much as fifteen feet; which meant that, as the hold was tidal, the men had to get the cases right on to the deck before they were safe. Some men, the more impetuous, arriving at the ship and finding the hold full, would plunge into the water, hoping to catch hold of a case and bring it to the surface. But inevitably they were choked and blinded by the oil and glad to be hauled out again. On his first trip MacMillan fell into the hold accidentally; he clawed for a handhold and eventually eased himself out. He was lucky; a length of calico had somehow wound itself round his legs and he might easily have been drowned.

Some of the old hands had as much as they needed after a few trips. Angus John reckoned his total haul as three hundred cases 'not to mention the odd bottles – they didn't count'. Norman MacMillan averaged about twenty cases a trip. John Curry and his mates averaged about eighty cases a night, his own share coming to over twenty. Some men, those with the larger boats, made a business out of the whisky; one is thought to have finished up with over a thousand cases. On the whole though, most men were content with a much more moderate figure. As the looting went on, however, there were rumours of police and Customs action, so a primitive system of look-outs was organized. Sometimes a boat was placed a hundred yards or so off, but usually the watching was done from the deck. Naturally in the darkness there would be false alarms, or wags would suddenly shout out 'Police coming!' then roar with laughter as their black-faced mates slipped and scrambled towards the rope ladder. The men in the boats would start shouting up, to ask what was happening, and the Tilly lamps would start shooting about in the darkness. There would be utter confusion; and order would not be restored till the joker was discovered or someone with a cooler head than his fellows had the wit to notice that no boat had arrived. Curiously enough, although in such panics men could get injured or even drowned, no one seemed to lose his temper. To most men this was the most exciting experience they had ever had in their lives and they were much too absorbed to indulge in recrimination. The only note of petulance was struck by the men of Eriskay – a secretive race at any time, who resented the intrusion of the other islanders. 'It's our boat,' they would say to men from the Uists or Barra, or Lewis; 'what the hell are you doing here?' 'Rescuing the whisky,' would come the sharp reply. To most Hebrideans the *Politician* did not belong to Eriskay; she belonged to anyone with the boat and the courage and the energy to reach her.

Norman MacMillan is full of stories at this time:

> I remember another night. It could be very quiet in the hold when the men were probing for the stuff . . . and the whole place was lit right round like a shrine. Thousands of candles on the wreck . . . and the Tilly lamps . . . and the place quite still while we

Arthur Swinson pictured on Eriskay in 1962.

The SS *Politician* in port. Gross tonnage was 7,939.
(Courtesy of National Museums Liverpool (Merseyside Maritime Museum))

Number Five Hold. Cases of whisky are seen at the back of the picture.
(Courtesy of Charente Ltd. (Harrison Archive at National Museums Liverpool, Merseyside Maritime Museum))

The stern of the SS *Politician* pounded by heavy seas. When it ran aground it was making fast headway at 17 knots. This shot, taken from a local's boat, shows how it dominated the landscape.
(Courtesy of Charente Ltd. (Harrison Archive at National Museums Liverpool, Merseyside Maritime Museum))

A collaborate venture. This grainy picture of Number Five Hold
suggests the team spirit.

The only known picture of Charles McColl (back view) on the deck of the SS *Politician* surveying the operations, bringing home how isolated he really was.
(Courtesy of Charente Ltd. (Harrison Archive at National Museums Liverpool, Merseyside Maritime Museum))

The *St Joseph*, the motor boat which was commandeered by Charles McColl to chase the looters. On deck is John, Archie McIsaac's son.

Lochboisdale on South Uist, photographed by Arthur Swinson in 1962 – little has changed since the 1940s.

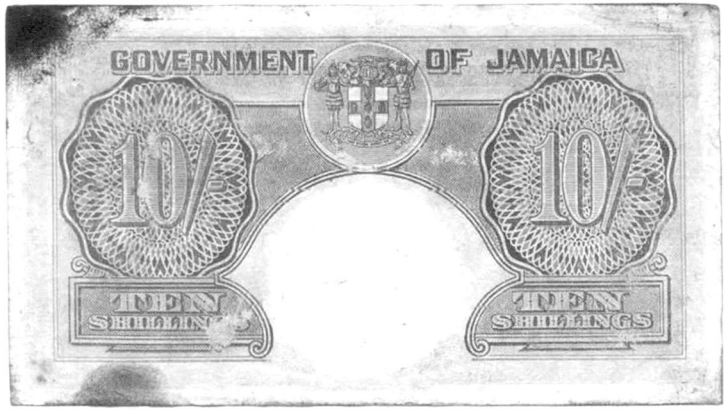

Follow the money... Jamaican ten shilling notes.
'Why was the currency stored among bales of cloth and cases of whisky?
The whole episode is very curious.'
(Reproduced with kind permission of Keith Hewitt.)

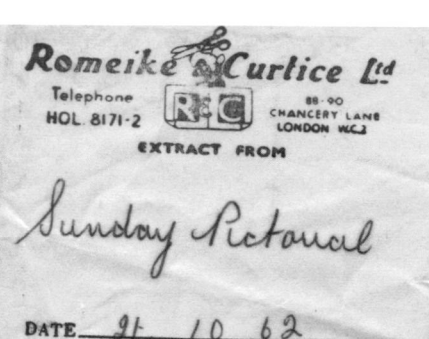

240,000 Scotch

- On February 3, 1941, the S.S. Politician (7,939 tons gross) sailed out of the Mersey for Jamaica and America, carrying whisky, huge sums of money, cars, bicycles and cloth.

  Early next morning she stuck fast on rocks off the Hebrides. To the local islanders, she was a gift from the heavens.

  A book by Sir Compton Mackenzie, a film and a song have been inspired by their wild antics.

  Now, for the first time, here are the full facts behind the Plunder of the Polly.

HERE, AT LAST, ARE THE FACTS ABOUT SCOTLAND'S MOST FAMOUS VICTORY

South UIST

ERISKAY

BARRA

Scotland's most famous victory? Review from the *Sunday Pictorial*.

probed. Then the engine room telegraph rang 'Full steam ahead' and everyone scrambled up the ladder. Some joker had been up to the bridge and found that the bell was still working.

Another day, someone shouted that the police launch was on the way. One of the boys was stripping off his oily clothes and he hadn't got dressed. In fact he was stark naked. The others were all ready and the launch was getting near so they had to go away and leave the poor man on the *Politician*. With the police right on him he didn't know what to do. He knew that they'd search right through the cabins, so in the end he hid in a ventilator. He was standing there naked for nigh on four hours while the police and the excisemen were looking around. And his hardest time was when one of these gentlemen came up against the ventilator. Well – I won't say what he did there – but it was all this boy could do to stop laughing.

Once a boat had got safely away from the *Politician* and reached land, there began the business of unloading the cases and carrying them across the machar, the belt of sandy dunes between the beach and the rock. Each man would ply between the boat and his hiding-place, carrying one or two cases at a time, his Tilly lamp held precariously to light the way. (Someone has said that there were so many lamps moving about the machar on a fine night that it reminded him of the Blackpool illuminations.) Having humped all the cases to their hiding-place, the next thing was to start digging – even in the machar not an easy job after a long row. You had to choose a spot which you could identify later on, and yet one which would not be too obvious to other people. If you left a mark of any kind, naturally the stuff would be gone before you had time to return to it. So men worked like ants, each one intent on burying his own treasure.

At the beginning, the majority of people without boats of

their own, or who could not find a place in one of the crews, began feeling out of things. The whisky was coming ashore, thousands of bottles of it, and it seemed there would be none for them unless they were willing to pay for it. Then they discovered that it was quite easy to get hold of *without* a boat. All they had to do was lie up in the machar and watch the burial parties in the early hours of the morning – then with the help of a spade, they could get as much whisky as they liked. Peter MacInnes told me he lost an entire load this way. A friend of Angus John's rowed his reserve stock out to a small island near Barra – probably Fuday – and buried all forty-six cases of it, against the day when he might run short. When he returned, only four cases were left. As Angus John put it: 'Some kind-hearted joker!'

Even when someone was left to guard the loot, things could still go wrong, as in this story from Norman MacMillan:

We had to leave the cargo on the rocks just below the jetty. One of the men stayed to watch it and we came home. Now there were two or three old women getting whelks in the rocks, and they decided to break off getting whelks and go in for whisky instead. When we went back the next night, there were fifteen cases short – out of forty-five.

But MacMillan bore no resentment against the look-out:

Well. . . he'd had a hard night's work and I dare say he'd taken a sample from one of the cases. He went asleep in the heather. When we got back to him the old ladies had taken his boots off – and they'd had a go at his trousers too.

Often people would forget the exact location of their cache and walk over the machar probing every yard or so. David Shaw, the Procurator-Fiscal at Lochmaddy, told me the story of a man who was admitted to Lochboisdale hospital very sick and needing a major operation. But every time the doctors asked him how he felt, his reply was, 'Don't you worry about me, how's my wee doggie?'

This went on till he came round from the operation, and again his first question was: 'How's my doggie?' Unfortunately news had come in that the dog had died and, as soon as it was thought fit, it was broken to him. 'No. . . no!' he said, 'that canna be. . . that *canna* be!' The Sister assured him that it was and lifting mournful eyes he said: 'If that's so, I don't want to live.' Upbraiding him for such foolish talk, the Sister asked why he had been so concerned about the dog while his own condition was so serious.

'Don't you understand?' he groaned. 'It's only the dog who knows where the whisky's hid in the machar!'

To say there was celebration on the islands would be something of an understatement. In the early days, life in some of the crofts was one long carousal. Parties blew up at the slightest excuse. Courting couples decided that this was the exact time to get married. Even chores like peat-cutting were turned into a festival, the parties getting through a crate a day. Old people, relatives and friends, were the recipients of unexpected gifts. Angus John told me:

I gave a lot to my friends. I never sold a bottle. I never gave a bottle either – I wouldn't insult people like that. I gave it away by the case.

For the first time, in fact, the crofters, who had lived hard and never possessed very much to be generous with, could be generous to the point of folly. People would go from croft to croft visiting their friends, hearing the latest news of the looting, and taking a dram before leaving. Every drink was prefaced by a toast to: 'The Captain of the *Polly* – God bless him.' Few had seen him, none (as far as I can tell) even knew his name, but apart from reigning monarchs, Captain Beaconsfield Worthington must be one of the most toasted men in the history of drinking.

Peat-cutting was a great time in those days. Norman MacMillan told me:

> A case a day was the usual go – twelve bottles. I mean the day we were cutting our peats and we had to get in a few people to help us. We'd give them all they wanted to drink – and a bottle to take home with them when they went away.

As everyone discovered, as soon as they tasted the whisky from the *Politician*, it was not any old stuff. It was the finest whisky that Scotland could produce, and though it was bottled under a hundred different labels it was not only as strong as the spirit they had been used to, it was even stronger. The bulk of it, of course, was in bottles of various shapes, including the elegant Haig 'dimples', but some was in large decanters, and the stoppers for these caused some confusion. They were an inch or so thick and four or five inches long, with an air bubble inside. Some of the islanders – not the brightest – imagined that they were small bottles, and, failing to discover the cork, attacked them with hammers. Father Morrison, the priest on South Uist, so I am told, came across a group so engaged, but no argument of his could persuade the men that they would find no whisky inside. Only after several stoppers had been reduced to splinters was the awful truth accepted.

In all communities, there is a lunatic fringe and the Western Isles are no exception. A small proportion of the men, there can be no doubt, went on drinking till their health suffered; some became confirmed drunkards. But the bulk of the people enjoyed the episode as a unique spree that would never be repeated. All their instincts for revelry and conviviality, for laughter and song, bubbled to the surface and turned life into a great carnival of the spring. As Angus John put it:

> It was a great thing we knew would never happen again . . . We enjoyed it while it lasted. We've enjoyed talking and thinking about it ever since.

To add to the carnival atmosphere were the dozens of bicycles which were landed with the whisky. Old people, who had never sat astride a saddle in their lives, had a go on them, and made a wavering course along the narrow roads, being hooted at by cars and shouted at by pedestrians. The children were, perhaps, even worse, trying to ride machines too big for their short legs. Some of the more enterprising began making up complete machines from the hundreds of spare parts which were landed. The children, especially the girls, had a wonderful time with all the perfume, and I was told that on Eriskay, especially, the school-room stank worse than a Bond Street beauty salon. A good deal of the perfume was contained in spray bottles and a favourite game among the children was to circle round, trying to spray each other in the face. MacGregor asserts that the air of gaiety was soured by a macabre note when the chickens got drunk from the dregs of whisky lying in the broken bottles on the machar. This may have been true of some hens; I could never find anyone in the islands who had actually seen one.

A more sinister development which can be verified, however, was the awakened commercial instincts of a few members of the community. It is extraordinary how, in any unusual circumstances, there are some people who can use them to make money. In prisons there have always been 'tobacco barons', and in the prison camps in Germany during the last war (so Aidan Crawley tells me) there were 'merchants', some of whom ended their captivity relatively wealthy. So it was on the islands in the spring of 1941. A few men, especially those with their own boats, began selling the whisky. Sir Compton Mackenzie told me he was offered three hundred cases at £2 a case – an offer he refused, not wishing to encourage such trade. The usual price was about ten shillings a bottle, and as some of the men were able to land three thousand or more bottles, it is obvious that the profit was not inconsiderable. During my stay on the island, Allan (the driver) pointed out to me a large house which he said had been built out of '*Polly* profits', as he called them. The merchants were fortunate in having an available market up at Benbecula, where some five hundred navvies were at work constructing the airport. At weekends some of these would make their way down to Loch-boisdale, brandishing notes and buying up whatever bottles they could get hold of, but, to save them the trouble, the merchants began running truck loads of whisky up to Benbecula. Wilson, the engineer, told me a delightful story of this period. One of the drivers taking a cargo north became aware that the police car was following him. Scared, he accelerated, only to arouse the suspicions of the police, and a chase ensued right up the island. There are few side roads and the driver knew that even if he turned down one of them he would soon be cornered, so the only thing was to keep going. He crossed the causeway over Loch Bee, went on over the South Ford, and on to Benbecula Island, the thirty cases hurtling to and fro in the back. Soon he gained a lead of about a quarter of a mile, though as the road was flat and straight the police car was still visible. Towards the north of the island he turned off left and made for the airport, hoping perhaps to find some navvies handy who would hide the stuff quickly, in the minute or so before the police arrived. But no one was around, only a great bulldozer pushing a mountain of hard-core over the foundation rubble on the runway. The driver swung his truck round and brought it to a stop by the bulldozer, dropped the tailboard, and flung the cases down on to the rocks. The bulldozer rumbled forward and in a matter of seconds the cases were hidden beneath three feet of hard-core. When the police arrived a few seconds later, the truck was empty and the driver went away free. But (so they say) even today, if you see a Scot mournfully contemplating the runway at Benbecula he is not looking for lost sixpences. He is thinking of those thirty cases of good Scotch whisky buried beneath the tarmac for ever.

It was, I suppose, about late April or early May that the mood went sour. To the majority of the islanders, to all reasonable men, the party had been wonderful but it had lasted long enough. The time had come to sober up and start work again. Such bottles as were left were hidden beneath the floor or in the walls or in the roof, there to wait for feast days, wedding or holidays. The normal pattern of life resumed its course; but, as it generally came to be realized, things were not quite the same.

To begin with, there was a split between those who had drunk the whisky or given it to their friends, and those who had traded in it. Angus John said proudly: 'I never sold a bottle.' Peter MacInnes said the same thing, as did Norman MacMillan and John Curry. But they could all name people who had gone in for selling. More serious, however, was the feeling between those who felt they had been informed against and the people whom they suspected of doing the informing. Curiously enough, the men whose whisky was stolen from its hiding-places in the machar or elsewhere seemed to bear no resentment at all. 'What did it matter?' Peter MacInnes said. 'It was all part of the fun.' This feeling, I believe, was general; the people who dug the cases out of the machar had no more right to them than the people who had lifted them out of the *Politician*. But as long as someone enjoyed the stuff, there was nothing to crib about. One could always go back another night and enjoy fishing in the flooded hold with a spear; the supply of whisky there was obviously limitless and the getting of it was only slightly less exciting than the drinking. But informing to the police or the Customs was quite another matter. This was treachery. This was stabbing a fellow islander in the back. Despite the native closeness of the islanders, ugly rumours began to circulate. . . of men being chased at sea, or being caught as they landed with their hauls. . . of police and Customs going from house to house searching. . . of men being arrested and sent to Lochmaddy for trial. Fear, suspicion, mistrust, began to stalk the islands. Men looked on their neighbours and began wondering which of them might be their betrayer. Divisions were to appear between man and man, between croft and croft, between old friends, and even between relations; divisions which even today have not been healed. Later on, there were to be further divisions between those who had been caught and punished and those who went scot-free. These, too, still exist.

But who was caught and how? And what was the charge against them? How many men were caught altogether? As I travelled among the islanders I continually asked these questions, only to receive vague answers. In fact I came to the conclusion that no one there knew the whole picture, only what happened to people near them. Fortunately, however, from the Customs documents in my possession I have been able to build up a complete picture.

CHAPTER 5

The Customs Counter-Attack

THERE IS A GENERAL BELIEF, held even by many of the islanders, that the *Politician* had been wrecked and the whisky looted for some weeks before the authorities became aware of it. MacGregor in his book says that after weeks 'the attention of the Ministry of Shipping and the Customs authorities was at last directed to Eriskay'. This, of course, is quite inaccurate. The Ministry of War Transport and the Ministry of Supply had copies of all signals sent out by the ship from the SOS onwards, and had, no doubt, given official instructions to the Liverpool and Glasgow Salvage Association who sent off Commander Kay and the *Ranger*. Also, Charles McColl had known of the incident within hours and had telephoned his superior, Ivan Gledhill, at Portree. From the 5th onwards the wreck had been McColl's chief concern. The police officer, Donald MacKenzie, was also in the know from the start. Whether one agrees that all the various authorities acted rightly or even sensibly, one cannot deny that they acted promptly.

Charles McColl, the principal figure of the tragi-comedy to be played out between the islanders and the authorities was a native of Mull, an island off the mainland of Scotland some several miles to the south east of South Uist. While not delicate, he was not a particularly strong man and suffered sporadically from a duodenal ulcer. Unlike the majority of people on the island who were Roman Catholic, he was a Presbyterian and for some time was treasurer of the church at Daliburgh. He was a quiet man, courteous and helpful. Norman MacMillan called him 'A real gentleman'. Ivan Gledhill told me:

Charles was held in great esteem by everyone; but if they did wrong he had no sympathy for them – he'd just go right ahead.

He was also a brilliant fisherman and, according to Gledhill 'Got more salmon in South Uist than anyone.' No doubt McColl was, to a certain extent, isolated from the community, not only because he was a foreigner and a Presbyterian, but because of his job. But he had lived in the Outer Hebrides for some years and had married there; and while they kept a weather eye on him, the islanders liked him, most of them even after the story of the *Politician* was over. Of all the people I questioned about him, only Angus John was harsh, saying: 'He did more than he need've done.' But one must recognize that Angus John's viewpoint was, shall we say, specialized.

When I began my researches I had been told at King's Beam House (the headquarters of the Customs and Excise Department) that Ivan Gledhill was still alive but in Kenya, and that a letter could be forwarded. To my surprise, however, the reply came from Wray, near Lancaster, and as soon as possible I arranged to go up there. It is a remote, delightful spot. You go up the Lancaster by-pass then turn off right. The road winds through the hills and the lush farming country for ten miles or so when you turn right again. Here the country becomes even hillier and, winding my way up a narrow canyon, I began to wonder if there was room for a house at all. But then the canyon widened into a valley and I found Gledhill's house next to an old mill, nestling on a green ledge above a trout stream called the Roeburn. Gledhill himself was already at the door as I drove up, and when I had got out of the car he was standing by it to greet me. 'I rejoice to see you,' he said. 'I rejoice to see you.' He led me into the house, introduced me to his charming wife, poured out some wine, and sat down to talk. At this time

I had only met one man (Huntington, the Second Engineer) who had been aboard the *Politician*, and even he had left it a few days after the accident. But here was a man who had followed the story through almost to the end – a man who had kept notes, diaries, and most wonderful of all, photographs. For the first time I was able to see what the *Politician* looked like, to examine her position as she lay on the rocks, and to hear first-hand stories of the efforts to free her.

Both McColl and Gledhill were members of the Outdoor Service of Her Majesty's Customs and Excise. Many people imagine that this great Department of State consists solely of the officers meeting returning voyagers at ports to ask them if they have anything to declare. These uniformed officers, in fact, belong to the Waterguard, the smaller branch of the Department. The officers of the Outdoor Service do not wear uniform and they deal chiefly, though by no means solely, with excise. A lot of their work is concerned with the old revenue trades such as distilling and tobacco manufacture. (As a rough definition, excise is duty payable on goods manufactured inside the United Kingdom, while customs (or customary dues) are payable on goods manufactured outside it). Her Majesty's Customs are a very old organization; there was a Custom House in London before it was the capital of England, and still governed by the Kings of Mercia. Even the Romans are said to have built their Custom House on the site of the present one. The Customs were established as a national organization as far back as the reign of King John; in 1204 he ordered that the customary dues should be accounted direct to the the State Exchequer thereby avoiding the clutches of the Sheriff and the Shire. Since Geoffrey Chaucer was Comptroller of Customs in the Port of London, the Department has always maintained a strong literary tradition; Robert Burns, Matthew Prior, Tom Paine, William Congreve,

Horace Walpole, Adam Smith and more recently, Richard Church, Neil Gunn, and Donald Giltanan, have all been excisemen. Technically the men of the Customs and Excise are civil servants, though they do everything possible to avoid the stock image. Personal eccentricity seems to be encouraged rather than deprecated, and ideas on clothing are decidedly nonconformist. I even met one excise officer, near retirement, who boasted to me that in all his years of service he had never worn a collar and tie. There are, of course, reasons for this attitude, the first being that there were Customs years, centuries even, before there was a civil service. Also the Customs officers (I am speaking of the Outdoor Service now) by the nature of their work must develop a sense of independence, and learn to do their job with a minimum of supervision. Charles McColl, for example, was separated from his superior by thirty miles of sea. Another characteristic of Customs men – that is in contrast to the orthodox civil servants – is their lack of officiousness or undue secretiveness. They will discuss their service and moan about the pay and, on occasion, the vagaries of their bosses in London who govern their lives. But there is one phrase which will bring them to their feet immediately and hurl them into action: 'Loss to the revenue.' There is nothing they will not do to prevent this, or to bring the culprits to book once it has occurred. It is like murder to a police officer; it has all the horror of a smallpox epidemic to a medical officer of health. Once one realizes this, one can understand immediately McColl's dismay when he learned the nature of the *Politician*'s cargo. Sooner or later the Scots and the Scotch would be bound to get together.

As already mentioned, Gledhill's orders to McColl were that he should 'take all necessary precautions for revenue security'. But when these orders were given there was still hope that the ship, once lightened, could be floated off the rocks and taken to

Glasgow. No one could foretell that on 12 March the salvors would desert her and she would lie there, an unattended wreck, for two whole months. The hatches were battened down and had the Customs seal affixed, but at this time nothing more could be done to protect the vessel. As McColl had pointed out, night-watchmen were almost unobtainable and would be unreliable even if they could be. All he could do, in fact, was keep his eyes open and listen. . . and it was not long before he had concrete evidence that not only had the Customs seal been violated, but also that some of the cargo had been successfully removed and brought ashore.

Some people on the island told me that the first inkling that McColl received was the sight of *Polly* bottles (as they were now called) littering the machar. They were not ordinary bottles such as one buys in shops in the United Kingdom; apart from their shape, they were embossed with lettering which read: 'Federal law forbids sale or re-use of this bottle.' As McColl already knew, the ship was on its way to the United States. Also, he no doubt observed the unusual air of revelry and the increasing drunkenness. So on 15 March he made arrangements to hire Archie McIsaac's boat, and that evening with the police constable from Lochboisdale, Donald MacKenzie, he sailed up the Sound of Eriskay towards the *Politician* and then passed it out into the Minch. Soon a sailing-boat was spotted, coming from the ship and sailing west, probably heading for Lochboisdale. McColl asked McIsaac to turn and overhaul it, which he was able to do in a few minutes and brought his boat, the *St Joseph*, alongside. At once McColl and MacKenzie could see that she was loaded with cases of whisky. There were eight men aboard but they tackled them quite fearlessly, took their names, and demanded that they hand over the whisky. The men did so without argument – all twenty cases. Their names were D A MacLeod, Angus

MacLean, Angus Morrison, Alex Macrae, Alex McIntyre, Donald MacNeil, Roderick Campbell, William MacDonald and Fergus MacKenzie. McColl noticed that apart from the whisky there were various other goods pilfered from the *Politician*, but before he could deal with them another boat was spotted coming from the wreck. The men aboard this boat, however, had already sensed that something was amiss and were heading east up the Sound as hard as they could go. Unluckily for them McIsaac's boat had the speed, and after a brief chase they were over-hauled. Aboard this boat were five men: Alex O'Henley, John Steele, Angus MacDonald, Donald MacNeil and Angus Macrae. Their haul was thirtyfive cases. Like the other crew, they surrendered without violence and McColl took his total capture – some sixty cases – to East Kilbride. Here he left Donald MacKenzie in charge and walked the two miles to the Pollachar Inn to telephone for a truck. While he was telephoning, however, he happened to look up and saw a third boat coming ashore. Immediately he rushed down to intercept it. There were six cases of whisky aboard and one of stout. The crew, no doubt cursing themselves for their ill-luck, were John MacAskill, Norman MacLean, John MacInnes, Donald Peter MacInnes, and Roderick MacMillan. It says something for McColl's moral authority that, despite the absence of any police support, he could make the islanders surrender their precious loot. Typically though, in his report he asks that the work of Donald MacKenzie should be brought to the notice of the Chief Constable, Inverness.

This had been a most successful night's work, but McColl did not blind himself to the true position; 'the pilfering of spirits and other cargo', as he called it, was going on apace, and for every boat he intercepted a hundred would get ashore. The area to be covered was vast, not only including South Uist and Eriskay, but all the islands of Barra. To control the situation effectively a whole regiment of Customs officers would be needed; but McColl was alone and would remain so. All he could do was his best. With regard to the offenders he had managed to catch, he told his superiors that salutory penalties were called for if and when proceedings were instituted. He hoped obviously that if an example were made of these men, others would be discouraged from looting. But the law was not in the hands of Her Majesty's Commissioners for Customs and Excise, and it moved at its own pace.

On 17 March, that is two days later, McColl and MacKenzie began searching the crofts of the men they had caught at sea. If they had any doubts as to the extent and variety of the looting, they were to be removed now. At Steele's croft, for example, they found such unlikely articles as washing soda, bed springs, a doormat and a cushion. In a barn behind the croft they did however find three bottles of whisky, but that was all. At another croft they found more bed springs and a tarpaulin. But later on their searches yielded great hauls of articles – mattresses, shovels, rolls of canvas and cloth. In the evening McColl and MacKenzie sallied forth again and searched Neil Campbell's croft, and were no doubt amazed at the articles that he had thought fit to bring home:

> six cakes of soap, three erasers, two boxes of rubber bands, and two notebooks, four lavatory-basin plugs, and chains, a bottle of ink, a tin opener, a potato peeler, a roll of bandage, a thermometer, three signal rockets, a roll of lamp wick, and some bottles of disinfectant.

Reading this list I can readily understand what Peter MacInnes meant when he remarked: 'There was everything a man could desire aboard that ship.'

Doggedly collecting together all these thousands of articles, large and small, McColl went searching the other crofts, but though he found something in each one of them he did not discover any whisky. Either the islanders' entire stock had been confiscated on the 15th, or the whisky was more carefully hidden than the other articles. No doubt he decided that the latter explanation was the more likely. The search took him to 22 March. He did not go out to the *Politician* at night, probably because he thought the weather was too rough to allow further looting. Here, in fact, he was wrong; but one has to remember that he had no boat of his own, being compelled to rely on Archie McIsaac's, and it is reasonable to assume that McIsaac was not anxious to risk his boat in relatively bad weather, even to please the Customs.

However, on 5 April McColl came to the opinion that the weather conditions were such as 'to encourage [as he put it] the return of the looters.' He therefore approached McIsaac for the boat, but for some reason it was not available. Perhaps McIsaac had his own views on the weather. McColl therefore had to adopt other tactics, so at 8.45 pm with MacKenzie, he went along the coast of South Uist past Ludag, that is on the north side of the Sound. Waiting here they saw two sailing craft coming from the *Politician*, one heading south for Eriskay and the other for South Glendale. There was nothing to be done about the first boat; all McColl could do was watch it sail slowly out of his clutches, loaded up to the gunwales with whisky and representing a considerable loss to the revenue, which must have sickened him. But with a little luck, he decided, he might intercept the second boat, and followed by MacKenzie he set off at a sharp pace. Later, in his report, he said that the interception:

> involved a walk over moor and bog of two and a half miles and it was questionable whether we could cover the distance before

the boat got in, but a low tide prevented it landing near the head of Glendale Bay where we had taken up position and lay concealed from view. Shortly after our arrival at the head of the bay we saw about half a mile away, figures against the sky, and watched three then walk along the side of the bay opposite towards that on which we were concealed. As they approached the head of the bay, we moved across towards them in the gathering dusk and walking on sand as we were, they were unaware of our presence till we spoke to them. One of them was carrying a sack but said nothing. The second man had moved towards the left and was intercepted by the police constable.

This passage, which occurs in a long report containing a mass of technical data, surely has some of the colour and romance of a Buchan story. One has only to compare it to the statement a policeman would have written, or indeed a civil servant of any other department, to realize what the long literary tradition has wrought in the Customs. McColl was obviously a man whose sense of language never deserted him, even in routine reports completed under pressure. The suspects (the third man had somehow disappeared in the darkness) turned out to be two boys, Joseph and John Peter MacInnes, and the sack they were carrying contained twelve bottles of Gilbey's sherry. Joseph freely admitted the theft and gave their names and address, but John Peter turned ugly and refused to give his address. McColl's attention was now drawn to the boat; as he suspected, it was loaded with more bottles of sherry. But the third man must have somehow got back to it and sailed it away in the darkness.

For the next few days McColl and MacKenzie concentrated their efforts on searching the crofts of South Uist, but with no great success. The early seizures had taught the islanders a lesson and nothing was left around which might incriminate them.

Whisky buried about the house was dug up and taken to a distance, to be buried again where the Customs could not reach it. Odd bottles were hung up chimneys, concealed in the thatch roofs, or in hollow walls. Angus John, as usual, was ready when they came to search his house. He told me:

> Donald MacKenzie came round and asked if I'd got aught from the *Politician*. I said that as he was here he'd better search the house. Well, he did, but not a drop did he find. I'd stacked all the bottles behind the wooden lining and he didn't think of looking there.

Some people were caught on the hop though, and had to use their wits. There is the story of the old lady on South Uist who, hearing a shout that the police were coming, put all her bottles in a heap in the yard and covered them with hay. Then she led her cow over and let it stand there munching contentedly. The police did not even give the heap a second glance. Another old lady (this story comes from Angus John) poured her bottles of whisky into the chamber pot and slipped it under the bed. The police did not suspect that either.

A good many of the stories are reminiscent of the troubles in Ireland, though they need not be any the less true for that. When communities want to hide something, their techniques are bound to be similar. Angus John and John Curry told me that on Eriskay some people were carousing, with a corpse in its coffin in the room next door. Getting word that McColl and MacKenzie were approaching they tipped the corpse out of the coffin and put it under the bed. The whisky bottles were piled into the coffin instead.

Norman MacMillan told me about an old lady that he knew – old ladies seem to have been particularly resourceful – whose croft was searched. As he put it:

There was a search on this day and the old lady, she hid the stuff in a wee haystack. As they were searching she got excited – she was watching them through her bedroom window. They went first to the peat stack and the old lady said 'You won't find it there.' Then they went over to a little cairn of stones. 'I'm still safe,' she said to herself. 'I'm still all right.' Then one of the police went over to the haystack and she cries: 'Oh, you so-and-so, you've got it at last!' She turned to find a policeman standing in the bedroom door, smiling at her. But he did not say anything – she was all right.

This story illustrates the point that the police did not have the same attitude as McColl. To him the looting was the most serious crime possible; it involved a loss to the revenue. To the police it was little more than petty larceny. Obviously the constable in this story was waiting to see if the whisky were found; if it was, then he would have to bring a charge. But if it was not, even though the old lady had given herself away, he had no wish to take action.

Norman MacMillan, as he put it, kept a weather eye on the police and McColl. 'I had so much of the stuff, I couldn't hide it,' he said. 'On my last trip alone my share was twentytwo cases – and several bags of bottles. They didn't count at all – they were just for the table. I often watched the police go by. . . and I was a bit anxious, I can tell you, with all that stuff about. But they never came in. I saw McColl sometimes and he tried to broach the subject, but I always changed it somehow. Talked about something else.'

Like the French Resistance a year or so later, the islanders made good use of elderly or sick relatives. Their hot-water bottles could be filled with whisky, and in case of real emergency a dozen or more bottles could be tucked around them under the blankets. To the islanders, now they knew that men were being charged and hauled off to Lochmaddy, McColl and MacKenzie and their occasional reinforcements were a serious menace. But as McColl knew only too well, the odds against him were immense. When he searched in South Uist, the whisky could be taken ashore on Eriskay or Barra, or any of a hundred small islands. But he went on relentlessly, searching the crofts, following up any bits of information by day, and trying to intercept the boats at night. He did not have any great success in this period; time after time he would find miscellaneous and trivial objects like bicycle parts, mattresses, or bed springs, but the vast haul of whisky which, as he knew, was still somewhere on the island, eluded him. This was not surprising, as the whole community was against him, firmly rooted in the belief that he was misguidedly trying to uphold a stupid law and condemn thousands of cases of good whisky to be polluted by salt water and wasted. Mrs McColl told me that he was out on the job for many hours at a time, and she was never sure when he would return home to eat or sleep, or how long he would stay. But neither the hostility of the people nor the weather could deter him, as he went on, risking his life in the treacherous peat bogs, or on the dangerous waters of the Minch. He emerges as a lonely figure, almost solely dependent on his own moral resources; but, if he had any doubts as to the validity of his actions, he certainly never showed them. As often as possible Ivan Gledhill would come over to give him support and accompany him on his journeys. But this could only be infrequently, as Gledhill's territory was vast, and other difficulties faced him, apart from the *Politician*. On one night alone, so he told me, he was called out of bed five times to deal with problems arising from ships which had run aground or been sunk or damaged by enemy action.

On Barra, the islanders had been bringing the whisky ashore

unmolested. Only four men had been caught and that was solely because one of them opened his mouth too much. The local constable knew they were selling the whisky on quite a large scale, but faced with concrete evidence he had to take action. The men's crofts were searched, and thay were charged with theft. I am obliged for this information to John McCormick who, at the time, was Compton Mackenzie's driver. He told me that no one was ever caught bringing the stuff ashore on Barra.

Early in April a salvage officer arrived from the Ministry of Supply and McColl took him out to the wreck. Here they found that a large quantity of china clay and salt was strewn all over the cargo decks, the islanders having taken the sacks it was stored in to carry the bottles. What was the object of the salvage officer's visit is not clear, but it may have been through him that a watchman was put aboard the ship. A more senseless move can scarcely be imagined. The watchman was ordered to go on board at daylight and stayed there till evening. He was not allowed to remain at night as there was still the danger (so the experts considered) that the ship might heel over. In the circumstances it is difficult to see why he was engaged at all, as the authorities must have known – or if they did not, McColl could have soon told them – that it was at night that the islanders came to do their looting. Also, as McColl had predicted two months earlier, the watchman proved unreliable. As Angus John put it: 'He was in the racket the same as us.' According to John Curry, he was taken off after a week or two, since it had been found that, far from protecting the whisky, he was merely giving priority to his mates on Eriskay. On 7 April McColl reported to his superiors that the looters had got away with not far short of one thousand cases. This figure quite horrified him, but, had he known, it was only a small fraction of the actual total.

On 12 April there was a very low spring tide and the weather was good, so McColl and MacKenzie hired a boat and made another of their night forays into the Sound. It appears that they sailed from Lochboisdale, approaching the *Politician* from the east, and as might have been expected, found boats thick around her. From his description this must have been the last night that Norman MacMillan was aboard. He says:

> The last time was the best of all. It was an extraordinarily low tide and you could walk in among the boxes. That night we handled one hundred and forty-four cases of the best!

If it was this night, MacMillan was lucky with his timing, for as McColl and Mackenzie approached they could see a boat leaving the *Politician* and making a course round the north of Calvay before heading for Eriskay. They set off in pursuit, but the boat reached the shore before they could get near it. Meanwhile they had spotted a rowing-boat and pulled up alongside. In it were three men, all covered with oil, but luckily for them there were no cases of whisky aboard. They must have been in the hold, however, as McColl realized, otherwise they would not have been covered with oil. (When I was up in the islands several people told me the story of a crew who had been forced to throw all their cases overboard before the Customs reached them, and this may well be the one. Whether they recovered the whisky later on, I never heard; but they may well have done, as the Sound is so shallow.) However, having drawn a blank with this boat, McColl headed for the shore and reached the sailing-boat before it could be unloaded. Here he seized seventeen cases of whisky and a dozen odd bottles. With the boat were three men: John Cumming, Alan MacMillan and Neil Gillies, all black with oil. MacKenzie asked them if they had been out to the *Politician* and one of them replied, 'Very likely.' They were all charged with theft – the first culprits from Eriskay to be brought to book.

Whether they had thought it might help their cause, it is hard to say, but they suddenly volunteered the information that a boat had just left for Lochboisdale, and if McColl left now he might just overhaul it. A more probable explanation is that they were determined, being caught themselves, that the interlopers from South Uist should not get away scot-free. Anyway, McColl decided to act on the information and after a chase of some three miles he overhauled the boat. It was stacked so high with cases that the gunwale was barely six inches clear of the water. There were fourteen cases and two hundred and twenty-five bottles aboard – a total of three hundred and eighty-three bottles. The crew consisted of four men: Neil Campbell, James Campbell, Colin McKinnon and Ronald MacDonald. The quantity of whisky was so great that McColl felt certain that they were intending to sell it, and, already suspecting that an illicit trade had been organized, he made arrangements with the police to man a check-point on the road north. Lorries were stopped and some seizures were made. But to man the point all round the clock it needed four policemen at least, and on South Uist there was only one, Donald MacKenzie. No doubt the merchants were watching him and as soon as he left to get a meal or some sleep the lorries would be rushed north to Benbecula.

Occasionally the police would get a tip-off when a truck was coming, but even this could not be relied on. When I met him at Lochmaddy, Mr Procurator-Fiscal Shaw told me that one morning MacKenzie was advised that the Army would be sending a convoy of twelve trucks to North Uist and that one of them would contain some cases of whisky He waited on the road, and dead on time the convoy appeared. Each truck was searched thoroughly, and when MacKenzie was right inside the last truck, a small lorry slipped past at speed, heading north for Benbecula. The merchants had known about the Army convoy and had used it as a decoy.

But McColl did have one hope; a report had reached him that the salvors would be returning on 26 April. Further, he had extracted a promise (I presume from the Ministry of Supply) that prior attention would be given to No. 5 hold and that the whisky would be sent under sealed hatches to Glasgow. If he could keep losses to a minimum meanwhile, there was still a chance that the bulk of the cargo would be saved. But there was another matter to be dealt with. It had come to McColl's notice that a large quantity of whisky was being sent off, a bottle at a time, through the post office to friends and relatives on the mainland. He reported this to Gledhill who immediately advised his superiors in London. A plan was devised to extract the offending parcels at the main sorting office in Glasgow; but before it could be put into operation word had got back to the post office at Lochboisdale. People coming to post bottles were tactfully advised to drink the whisky themselves.

21 April arrived but there was no sign of the salvors; and indeed it may well be that McColl was advised at this time that they would not be returning at all. The people who would be coming were the shipbreakers, and as he doubtless knew, they would have little interest in the cargo. Possibly it was this news which caused him to try and cope with the situation on Eriskay, where the whisky was pouring in night after night in vast quantities. He went across with Donald MacKenzie and they recovered a few items and four cases of whisky – but that was all. Frantically he searched crofts and barns and haystacks and went over the machar probing, but the loot still eluded him. As he reported later, the whisky was buried out in the machar or even taken to other islands. Wherever it was, he certainly could not reach it.

It was when he returned from this trip to Eriskay that McColl must have realized the strength of the islanders' feeling against him. He had been threatened, as had Gledhill, but Customs officers (sometimes wrongly) always imagine that they are immune from physical violence. However, in the early hours of the morning he was awakened by some fishermen who had just come into Lochboisdale harbour and seen a blaze. It was his garage. Someone had made a hole in the roof, poured some paraffin on to the car beneath, and put a match to it. If the fishermen had not chanced to come in at this moment the fire may well have spread to the house, with results that one can only conjecture. Actually, though the incendiaries did not realize this, there were two cars in the garage and McColl's escaped. But it was evident that a good many islanders shared Angus John's view that 'McColl had done more than he needed to'. Gledhill was very much concerned about McColl's safety, as were the King's Commissioners in London. The situation was aggravated by the fact that a number of men were back from Lochmaddy, particularly those he had caught on the night of 15 March. They had made their first appearance before the Sheriff and were now awaiting trial. McColl was, in fact, surrounded by a whole island of resentment, suspicion and hatred; but he refused to change his policy or to slacken his efforts. Every time he saw a *Polly* bottle lying in the gutter or out on the machar, the words 'loss to the revenue' must have beaten in his brain. And so he went on, and from all that anyone could judge, quite unafraid.

It was not until 12 May that the shipbreakers arrived. The contract for the west of Scotland was held by the Iron and Steel (Salvage) Corporation who sub-contracted the job to Messrs Arnott, Young of Glasgow. Their consultant engineer, who took charge of the job, was Mr P E Holden, who arrived aboard the *Assistance*.

Noticing mention of the shipbreakers in the Lloyd's telegrams I had for some time been trying to find out who they were, but it was not until I was chatting to Wilson, the engineer, at Lochboisdale that I stumbled across a clue. One of the engineers on the job, he told me, had been a Duncan McIver who now had an office in Stornoway. Relying on the kindness of the GPO to look up his exact address, I posted off a letter, to receive a reply telling me about the Iron and Steel (Salvage) Corporation, Messrs Arnott, Young, and Holden. An inquiry to the first produced a formal reply that they had no records of the operation. A letter to Holden via Arnott, Young was more fruitful, and I arranged to go up to Scotland to meet him. He lived in Kippen, and as I had business in Edinburgh we arranged to have lunch at The Golden Lion in Stirling. He turned out to be a giant of a man with the most powerful shoulders I have ever seen except on a professional heavyweight, and he was soon producing photographs and data of all kinds. Much of it belongs to the later stages of the story but as, soon after his arrival, he made contact with McColl and Gledhill, it has been necessary to introduce him here.

Holden, or rather his employers, viewed the *Politician* from one angle only: as a supply of steel. Their object was to lighten her, seal her up a section at a time and pump in air, float her off the rocks and tow her to Lochboisdale. From there she could be towed to Rothesay and cut up into convenient sections for onward transmission to Troon. They lightened her in two ways; by removing cargo, and dismantling the superstructure – funnels, deckhouses, derricks, masts, and finally the upper decks. But if Gledhill and McColl hoped that their problems regarding the whisky would be solved immediately by Holden and his men, they were again doomed to disappointment. Holden did most certainly take off the great majority of cases still remaining, but they were not his primary concern and the job took some months. Meanwhile, as his men had to quit the ship at night (just as the salvors had done) the looting could continue as before. The fact that the cases still left were tucked away in inaccessible corners of the hold, often fifteen to twenty feet below the slime, did not worry the islanders; unlike Holden, they had all the time in the world.

Some of the whisky, as might be expected, was disappearing down the throats of Holden's men. One morning he heard a crash and looked round to see that a bottle had smashed itself to pieces behind him on the deck. Its owner was working up aloft and had somehow let it slip from his pocket.

Soon after his first meeting with Holden, Gledhill went round with McColl to seize the boats which had been going to the *Politician*. They were identified by name – informants having come in to McColl – and also by the fact that they were covered with fuel oil. The seizure was more symbolic than anything. An arrow was painted on the boat and the owner was warned formally that he must not use it for any purpose whatever unless advised further. Curiously enough – and certainly to Gledhill's surprise – no one having had his boat thus marked used it till the ban was lifted.

For some time Gledhill had been trying to get the police organized for a sweep across Eriskay; and on 5 June he succeeded. An inspector from Lochmaddy turned up, together with Sergeant MacDonald of Barra, Donald MacKenzie of South Uist and from the Customs two men from Stornoway, apart from Gledhill and McColl. They motored down to Ludag and boarded the *St Joseph*. Gledhill told me:

> It was one of the most amusing things you ever saw. No sooner had we crossed the Sound and landed on Eriskay than we spotted the people running about like rabbits carrying their precious cases of whisky. They were heading for the moors or the peat

bogs trying to hide the stuff before we could catch up on them. You never saw such activity. Of course, they were too late. Wherever we went we got tons of the stuff, whisky and other goods. By 1 pm we had to call the search off and it took us the rest of the day to get it over to Lochboisdale. There it filled the cells, the police garage, and the policeman's house. A lot of it had to be stacked outside.

I heard a lot about this stack by the policeman's house when I was up in Lochboisdale. To Angus John and others it symbolized all the stupidity of the law and authority. Someone would eventually acquire the whisky and drink it, they reasoned. Why should the men who had rescued it from the sea be penalized?

But to return to the search itself. Cases were found in stack-yards, in flower-beds, in outhouses, in the shore and in the peat. The search was continued a second day and a third, the haul mounting steadily. Dozens of people had had their names taken and were fearful of arrest. The more fortunate occupied their nights getting the last remnants of loot out of their houses and burying it so far up in the hills that no police officer or Customs man could possibly find it. Some took their precious cases in boats and rowed them out to the surrounding islands. Sunday came – but no police or Customs. This was a welcome respite, but Monday was awaited with apprehension. If the search were to go on much longer there would be no knowing what would be found. But fortunately a storm blew up, making the Sound too rough for the mail-boat to cross. On Tuesday the weather moderated, but the police and the Customs did not come back. In fact they never did. What had happened, of course, was that Gledhill had to release his men and the police inspector had to return to Stornoway to continue his normal duties. But the operation was not without results. The men of Eriskay began wondering if further trips to the *Politician* would be worthwhile. Much better, they thought, to spend the time conserving the stuff they had got already.

There was also a feeling that the party was nearly over. Apart from the suspicion and mistrust between croft and croft, already mentioned, there was one overriding fact, an event which had shaken the small communities of the islands as nothing had done since the arrival of the Viking longboats. Slowly people realized that many of the men who had come back from Lochmaddy, after their first appearance before the Sheriff, had gone back there for trial. By no means all of them had returned, and the news was that they had been sent to the mainland as convicts and were now serving sentences in the gaol at Inverness.

CHAPTER 6

The Law in Lochmaddy

AT THE BEGINNING OF my researches, I had learned that a number of looters had been dealt with at Lochmaddy, a note to this effect being included in the Customs records. But how many men were dealt with and what sentences they were awarded, no one could tell me. I therefore made contact with the Lord Advocate's Department in the Secretary of State for Scotland's office in Whitehall, and here a charming lady offered to contact her colleagues in Edinburgh, asking them to search for the court records. She was not very hopeful, however, and warned me that even if the records were found there was no guarantee that I should be allowed to inspect them. As it turned out, not a single reference to any looting case could be found in Edinburgh, the lady ringing back to say, 'If they're anywhere at all, they must be in Lochmaddy.'

'What sort of court have they got there?' I asked.

'I'm afraid no one seems to know. After all, it's terribly. . .' She paused, searching for a word. 'Terribly remote up there. We've no idea what goes on at all.'

Abandoning official sources for the moment, I turned to the Press for help; but a letter to the editor of the *Stornoway Gazette* produced a reply that a search through his files had not turned up a single reference. The *Glasgow Herald* and The *Scotsman* could not help me either, so I directed my efforts to discovering whether there was a free-lance journalist on South Uist or Barra. Here I drew another blank, so the next step was to search the reference books and, if possible, obtain some details of the law officers. This trail proved more successful, an entry giving not only the address of the court house, but also the names and titles of those concerned with it. They were a Sheriff Substitute, a Sheriff's Clerk, and a gentleman enjoying the title of Procurator-Fiscal. Uncertain of my welcome from Sheriff or Fiscal, I wrote to the Clerk but received no reply, and so I was still no wiser when I boarded the plane for Benbecula. It might be, I decided in my depression, that the reference book was wrong; or that the court had long ceased to exist. If it was as remote as the Lord Advocate's Department thought it was, anything might have happened. Still, whatever the truth, I had to discover it, and one of my first jobs on arrival was to ring the court house. After speaking to a police constable and being asked to hang on, then speaking to a police sergeant and being asked to hang on, a confused babble of voices came down the line, eventually (to my great relief) to be cut short by an authoritative voice saying: 'David Shaw, Procurator-Fiscal speaking.'

'Good morning,' I said. 'My name is Swinson.'

'Oh yes – you wrote to the Clerk, didn't you? I'm sorry you didn't get any reply but I was away and no one knew what to do about your letter.'

'What is the position then? Do you think you may have any records?'

'I have no idea – I wasn't here during the war. When do you propose to come up?'

'Tuesday morning.' (It was Saturday, then.)

'Very good. I'll search the archives over the weekend and see what I can turn up for you.'

Ringing off, I was relieved to find somebody willing to help me; but at the same time I could not help marvelling how effectively the passage of a mere twenty-one years had buried every phase of this story. With the Lord Advocate's Department's description of the court in my mind, I visualized a wooden hut rather of the kind one sees in Westerns, with no one writing down a word of the trial, not even the sentence. The mention of such unlikely characters as a 'Sheriff Substitute' reinforced this impression.

As it happened, Colonel Cameron was travelling up to visit his other factory on North Uist and he kindly offered to give me a lift to Lochmaddy, which lay between fifty and sixty miles to the north. Delighted to be spared the bus journey, I clambered into his estate car and we set off about 8.30 am immediately after I had settled my hotel bill. For the fifth day in succession the sun was still shining in a cloudless sky, and my eyes, now well accustomed to the Hebridean scene, could gaze on lochs and skerries and mountains with a warm appreciation. Even the silence had ceased to be hostile. The Colonel chatted pleasantly as we drove along, pointing out a landmark there, slipping in an anecdote or recounting the history of the place as if it had all happened yesterday. 'There,' he would say, 'that's one of the finest trout lochs in Scotland. They're sending up some helicopters next month to spray gravel on the bottom. . . That's the old castle of the Clanranalds. It was burned down when they were away at the '45. . . the last of the Clanranalds died in 1945. There's a co-lateral descendant in London still living though. . . I don't know what he's doing.'

We went on to talk of Culloden and the break-up of the clans. 'It was a medieval system,' he said. 'But it worked. The highlands have never been the same again.' We passed a large building which, he said, was the syndicate house, used by Colonel Greig and his associates when they came over from the mainland. Farther north we could see some RAF huts way over on the left. 'That's the rocket range,' he told me.

At the South Ford we could see some LSTs (Landing Ships,

Tank) at anchor, and by the road some RAF drivers were landing great trucks. The Colonel jerked his head towards them. 'Makes you think of D-day, doesn't it? Combined Ops and all that.' The same thought had crossed my mind. The last time I'd seen LSTs waiting offshore was on the Morib beach landing in Malaya at the end of the war – an experience I'd been trying to forget. We went on north over the Queen's Causeway linking South Uist, Benbecula, Grimsay, and North Uist. Said the Colonel: 'This was opened by the Queen Mother eighteen months ago. It's a wonderful job, and it's certainly improved life in the islands no end. Look at that little place – Grimsay. Till a couple of years ago it was as remote as hell. Now it's on the main road and they've even got a petrol pump. But the sense of adventure has been lost, all the same. In the old days, you see, you had to find your own way over the sands – and if you didn't know your stuff, you could soon get into the quicksands.' Already his mind was reaching back. 'I've been across the North Ford in every conceivable way – on foot, on horseback, car, Land Rover and a combination of all of them. . . but it does save time this way, if you're on business.'

It was a wonderful journey; sometimes we would seem to leave the land altogether and ride the narrow causeway with the sea on both sides of us. We would reach an islet, skirt one side of it, then take to the sea again, only to link with the right flank of an island farther on. Circling above us were gulls and seabirds of all kinds, and the air was salty and strong.

On North Uist the road forks, and we made a right incline towards Lochmaddy which lay some eight miles ahead. 'God knows what you'll find there,' said the Colonel. 'I don't think they're too well organized.' The hold of the land grew more and more tentative, and the road seemed to dance between the lochs and pools. Every hundred yards or so it seemed that there would not be sufficient room left for it to thread even the most tortuous passage, but somehow it always did. At about eleven o'clock we made a sharp right turn and ran down through a group of houses and shops on the fringe of a deep bay. This was Lochmaddy. The Colonel pulled up outside a newsagent's shop, saying, 'This is where he lives.' I took my baggage and tape-recorder and put them on the pavement, thanked the Colonel for all his kindness and help, and turned to face the building. 'The Weehavit Shop', I read, 'MacAskill and Shaw'. Could this, I wondered, be the abode of a Procurator-Fiscal? Inside, a blonde in a royal blue sweater was standing behind a counter stacked with newspapers and magazines, serving a postman. Hearing my name, she picked up the phone to tell Mr Shaw I had arrived, and soon I was being escorted through the back of the shop and up the stairs to the living quarters. Mr Procurator-Fiscal turned out to be a tall, lean, bespectacled man in the kilt of the MacIntosh clan, and he led me into his sitting-room. It was a comfortable room with a magnificent view of Loch Maddy and the mountains to the south of it. Briefs and bundles of legal papers in pink ribbon were littered about the table, chairs and floor, mixed up with such items as whipped cream walnut cartons, invoices, and display material. Following my gaze, Shaw smiled. 'I'm a part-time Fiscal,' he said. 'The only one, as far as I know, in the whole of Scotland. When I'm not doing this job, I'm helping with the business.'

He was not apologizing; he was explaining. Not, so far as I was concerned, that there was anything to apologize for. The man was obviously something of an original, living his own life in the way that suited him best. I admired him for it, as later on I was to admire his deep love and knowledge of the law. But now we were seated by the fire and I was asking apprehensively what had been the result of his searches over the weekend. Picking up some tomes from the floor and opening them on his knee, he said:

'It's been the devil of a job I can tell you. I had to spend hours in all those cupboards up at the court.'

'And what did you find?'

'I found the register, the charge sheets, and the sentences.'

'Any account of the proceedings?'

'No – none whatever. And I should doubt very much if they exist – or ever did.'

I explained that so far I had been quite unable to trace any newspaper accounts of the cases, and asked if he could help me here; but he shook his head.

'You can take it from me, at that time, in the war, there would have been no reporters here. They don't come even now, although we sometimes have some very interesting cases.'

So the last hope of any detailed account of the trials was gone; but at least records of the charges and the sentences existed. I asked, not without apprehension, what was the position regarding them.

'The rule is,' he explained, 'that I can only give you what came up in court. That means the names, the charges and the sentences.'

'What about the statements? They must have been brought up too?'

'I'm afraid I'll have to ask the Lord Advocate about them.'

'Well, could I have the names, charges, etcetera, now?'

'Certainly.'

With this information and the documents already in my possession from the Customs, I still might trace each story right through. The main deficiency of the Customs documents – from my point of view – was that they did not mention any names. But there was just a chance that if I put the two sets of information together the jigsaw would suddenly fall into place.

While we were talking, the police rang up to say they had two criminals – boys who had been damaging plant at a building site.

'When would you like to bring them up?' asked the Fiscal. 'Would twelve noon suit you?'

'Yes, sir,' said the policeman at the other end.

'Right. If you'll tell the Sheriff, I'll get the charge typed out.'

Excusing himself, he went over to the desk, pushed the invoices and cartons to one side, and began typing. Though frustrated at this delay now that I had almost got my clutches on the material I had been searching for so long, I nevertheless found myself fascinated at this inside glimpse of the operation of the law.

'Would you like to come down to the court?' the Fiscal asked as he finished typing.

'Yes – very much.' We got into his old car and took the road towards the north of the bay. Half a mile on another ancient model came rattling towards us, the sight of which caused the Fiscal to jam on his brakes and begin signalling through the window with his right hand. A hand came out of the other car, waving an acknowledgement, and soon it screamed to a halt alongside us.

'Good morning, Governor,' said the Fiscal. 'Have you heard – we've got a couple of criminals.'

'No, I hadn't,' said the other.

'The police have just been on. We're having a court.'

'When?'

'Twelve noon.'

'All right – I'll be there.' There was a revving of engines and the two rattle-traps lumbered forward in opposite directions.

'That's the Sheriff Substitute,' said the Fiscal. 'He runs the Poor Law Institution here. We've got two others – one is headmaster of the school and one runs a hotel. But I don't like worrying them at short notice, unless I have to.'

Soon we were at the court house, which turned out to be not

of wood at all but of stone, and a solid, imposing building at that. Inside, the Fiscal showed me the court-room and asked me to wait while he got things ready for the hearing, so I sat down on one of the wooden benches in the seven rows reserved for the public. For a court, it was a pleasant room with large pointed windows and a ceiling of Cambridge blue. Like the whole of the building it was spotlessly clean, the paint and the varnish shining and the floor so scrubbed that you could eat off it. This, I reflected, gazing at the Sheriff's bench, the dock, and the Fiscal's table, was the remotest court in the whole of the British Isles, a court so remote that not even the Lord Advocate's Department could say what it was like or what went on in it. It would be intriguing to see how justice was administered here.

Ten minutes later a police constable ushered in the accused, a couple of poorly-dressed lads, and put them in the dock. The Fiscal entered, still dressed in his kilt and jacket, and took his seat. Then a police sergeant suddenly appeared, yelling 'Court!' The Fiscal, the accused, the police, and myself stood for the entry of the Sheriff Substitute, who climbed up to his high seat and bowed. We bowed back and then all sat down again. The Sheriff called on the Fiscal to read the charge, which he did – a joint charge against both boys, whom I will call A and B. Having finished reading, the Fiscal then announced that 'The Prosecution is deserting the case against B' and proceeded to read a re-framed charge against A. B was released from the dock by the police sergeant, while the Sheriff explained to the remaining accused that this was a first hearing and that the case would be continued at a later date. Meanwhile he was advised to make arrangements for his defence and would be allowed free on payment of £10 bail. The accused, however, explained that he could not obtain the bail unless he could go free in the first place. Asked why not, he said:

'If I go back to my family they'll give me the money. But they won't bring it here.'

A short conference ensued between the Fiscal and the police sergeant, after which the Fiscal said he had no objection to letting the boy go, 'in the special circumstances'. The Sheriff, a round, bald-headed Pickwickian character, seemed relieved that such a weighty problem should have been resolved so speedily, and agreed to let the boy go. The police sergeant arose to yell 'Court!' and as we stood up again the Sheriff bowed and walked out. The proceedings were over.

As I went out to find the Fiscal I began pondering on the extraordinary depth to which the law has penetrated the culture of our islands. Here in this remote spot, were a part-time Sheriff, a part-time Fiscal, and two policemen administering justice with all the dignity of the High Court and, I felt sure, with the same fairness and meticulous regard for detail. If the Law – in the form of the Lord Advocate's Department – had forgotten them, they had certainly not forgotten the Law.

Back at his house the Fiscal entertained me to lunch, at which we talked of Scottish law and the differences between it and English law. He seemed to have studied the subject deeply, and ended by saying, 'If we could somehow get an amalgam of both systems we might have the most perfect law on earth.' He then went on to talk about the mountains which we could see from the window and told me that there was still deer on them, though the size of the beasts was going down. He told me the story of various occasions when he had hunted them, but added, 'I don't go out with a gun any more. It's more fun with a camera.' He also told me that there were still eagles nesting on the west of the island.

Then we got down to the documents. When he was doubtful

as to whether he could properly show me one, he put it to one side until such time as he could consult the Lord Advocate's Department, but meanwhile he read out the charge sheets. It appeared that all the looters were charged with the Common Law crime of theft. In the Customs papers there was some indication that a more serious charge had been mooted; but certainly it was not pursued. Shaw explained to me that in his view – and in the view, so he said, of most Fiscals – he would not proceed under a statutory charge if a Common Law charge could be used.

The first cases to come up were from Barra: Peter MacDonald and three others who first appeared on 26 April and were continued in custody until the 30th. They pleaded guilty and were fined, two of them £5 and two £3. Another man from Barra, Johnathan MacDonald, came up on the 30th but the prosecution deserted the case against him and he was dismissed.

On 13 May was the case of the four men whom McColl and MacKenzie had caught in the sailing-boat on 12 April after that tip-off from the men caught landing on Eriskay. They were Colin McKinnon, James Campbell, Ronald MacDonald and Neil Campbell. Neil Campbell had already been 'shopped' by an informer and his parents' croft searched. A whole mass of stores had been found there. But the case against him was found 'non proven,' as were the cases against McKinnon and MacDonald. James Campbell, however, was sent to prison for six weeks. Why this should be, it is impossible to say. Campbell was a young private in the Cameron Highlanders home on leave, whereas Colin McKinnon was a lorry-driver for a company engaged at Benbecula airport; at 48 he was much older than the other three. The four men were all (literally) in the same boat and must have expected to be awarded the same penalty. Though Campbell took the blame for his mates, it is difficult to see how his sentence was justified.

On the same day, 10 June, there began the trial of the nine

men in the first boat McColl and MacKenzie had caught on the night of 15 March. They were charged with the theft of twenty cases of whisky, thirty-one bundles of cloth, and sundry items such as bicycle tyres and matches. Again although they were all in the same boat, six of them (Donald MacNeil, Angus MacLean, Alex Macrae, Alex McIntyre, Angus Morrison and Fergus MacKenzie) received sentences of two months, Donald MacLean one month, and William MacDonald was fined £10. Roderick Campbell was let off altogether, the verdict being 'non-proven'. In the latter case it could not be proved that he had gone aboard the *Politician*.

On 11 June came the trial of the two boys McColl had caught coming ashore near Ludag in his Buchanesque adventure on the night of 5 April. John MacInnes was fined £3 and the case against his brother was dropped on account of his youth. Also on 10 June, James Morrison of South Uist was charged with reset, that is, receiving stolen property (three bundles of cloth and a pail). He was found guilty and fined £3.

On the same day the three men from Eriskay (John Cumming, Alan MacMillan and Neil Gillies) were tried, the charge being the theft of seventeen cases and ten bottles of whisky. They were awarded thirty days each. After this came the case of Donald Morrison, who plead guilty to the pathetic charge of stealing 'a bag of washing, two bread strings, a mattress, a bundle of canes, and a shovel', all these items being found at his house. He pleaded guilty and was fined £3.

10 June was obviously a busy day; eighteen islanders were tried and fourteen of them sentenced.

Three days later on 13 June the five men who had landed with a boat at Pollachar to be caught by McColl, came up for trial. Their names were John MacInnes, John MacAskill, Norman MacLean, Donald Peter MacInnes and Roderick MacMillan, the charge being the theft of six cases of whisky and one of stout. They pleaded 'not guilty'. Roderick MacMillan was found not guilty and the verdict on the others was 'non-proven'. Considering that they were caught red-handed, this seems most surprising, and the only explanation one can think of is the custom under Scottish law to require corroborative evidence. Unfortunately for him, McColl was on his own, MacKenzie having stayed to guard the other seizures. Nevertheless there was still the whisky to account for, and the defence must certainly have thought up a wonderful story.

On 8 July, Angus MacLean (who should have appeared with his eight companions on 10 June) appeared before the court and was sentenced to two months' imprisonment. On the same day Donald Morrison, charged with stealing two bottles of whisky, was fined £5. After him, three other men came up, their crofts having yielded up various stores from the *Politician* when they were searched by the police. On 12 June four of the men in the second boat caught by McColl on 15 March had come up for trial, charged with stealing fifteen cases of whisky. Alex O'Henley and Angus MacDonald were fined £5, Donald MacNeil and John Steele were sentenced to thirty days' imprisonment. Angus MacLean did not appear and the case against him was dropped.

Altogether by the time the last case had been disposed of, forty men had appeared before the court, thirteen of whom were given prison sentences. (Six for two months, one for six weeks, one for one month and five for thirty days.) Thirteen were fined. In nine cases the verdict was 'non-proven'. Three cases were deserted by the prosecution. One case was disposed of under the Probation of Offenders Act, and one man was found not guilty. Of the forty men charged, five came from Barra, three from Eriskay and thirty-two from South Uist. Considering that it is generally agreed that the bulk of the Whisky went to

Barra and Eriskay, these figures seem out of proportion and can only be accounted for by the fact that McColl himself lived on South Uist. The quantity of whisky covered by the charges was minute, compared to the total haul – less than a hundred cases.

My first reaction, having examined the details of each case, was surprise at the small number of men given prison sentences. Going round the islands I had imagined that the number must have been much larger – fifty or even a hundred. It seemed incredible that such relatively soft measures should have provoked so much bitterness and dissension. But, as the Fiscal was to explain to me, for an islander the very fact of being taken from his home as a criminal, to be shipped to the mainland, is a terrible affront to his pride. Some people, notably Alasdair Alpin MacGregor, have argued that the sentences meant little or nothing to the islanders, and they came back from Inverness grinning all over their faces, having had a wonderful time, sewing mailbags and recounting their experiences to the soft-hearted warders. From my own researches on the islands and certainly on the word of the Fiscal, this is quite untrue. Imprisonment would have been bad enough if the crime had been admitted; but the islanders admitted no crime, and the result of the sentences was therefore to infuse a growing sense of bitterness against the authorities.

The islanders' view of the wreck, as Angus John put it, was: 'Once the salvors quit a ship – she's ours.' This is the view, they have held for generations, though legally, one has to admit, they have not a leg to stand on. Section 536 of the Merchant Ship Act (1894) forbids the taking away of any cargo or part of a ship stranded. Dutiable goods are covered by Section 45 of the Customs and Excise Act (1952). Therefore by taking such items as bed springs, mattresses, washing soda, etc., the islanders were guilty of theft; by taking spirits they were also guilty of defrauding His Majesty of duty. But if the islanders had not the law behind them, one must admit that they had logic.

Since the arrival of the *Ranger* on 10 February they had watched the salvors at work taking off cargo. This work – interrupted by gales – had gone on for over a month till 12 March when they had finally left. Some hundreds of tons of cargo had been salvaged and the islanders assumed, quite rightly, that as the whisky was not taken it was not wanted. It is even conceivable that Commander Kay's reply to Huntington may have reached them: 'It's not worth the effort.' They were certain that if they did not rescue the whisky, it would be lost for ever.

It has been suggested in some quarters that the islanders conveniently adopted this viewpoint after the wreck of the *Politician* to salve their own consciences, but this is not true. As Ivan Gledhill put it:

> It goes back for generations . . . always in the islands they have regarded a wreck as their own property. Though I cannot approve, I can sympathize.

It will not do either to condemn this belief as a general token of their dishonesty. Gledhill told me that in his long experience of them the islanders proved to be very honest indeed. Mr Procurator-Fiscal told me:

> You can leave any mortal thing around and they won't touch it. The only exception is spanners – don't leave them about.

Another point is, in my view, the feeling of all islanders that a wreck is some sort of bonus or compensation for the lonely, hard, and often impoverished lives they have to lead. Angus

John had this thought in mind when he said: 'There was everything aboard that boat a man could desire'. Or Peter MacInnes, when he said: 'It was a cargo from heaven'. This general attitude to wrecks applies no matter what is aboard them; but when the cargo is whisky, one must recognize the fact that another dimension comes into the picture.

The word 'whisky' is Celtic and comes from the Gaelic *Uisgebeatha*, the water of life. Its origin is shrouded in the Celtic mists but it must surely be almost as old as Scotland herself. For anyone who does not know, the spirit is distilled from fermented barley, and an essential ingredient is the water that has come 'off peat'. Though the distilling process is simple in essence – and can be carried out in the humblest croft – it is surrounded by ritual and legend. If a still has to be replaced, so I was told up on Speyside, it will be copied right down to the dents. Whisky started out as a drink of the people – Robert Burns called it 'the poor man's wine' – when the court was still drinking claret, but by 1500 it had reached the King's table. It was greatly loved by James IV who fell at Flodden. It sustained Prince Charles on the March of '45 and fortified him in the disasters which followed.

Before Culloden a duty of 2d. a gallon had been imposed from London but the Highlanders ignored it. Afterwards however, the Government tried to control the distribution of whisky and sent up excise men (known as gaugers) to assess the duty, then 9s. 6d. per gallon. The Highlanders replied by smuggling, and illicit stills flourished, which the Government were powerless to stamp out. A law was brought in forbidding distilling in stills of under five hundred gallons, and this the Highlanders defied too. By 1820 illicit distilling had become so rife that a move was made to change the law. In 1823 an Act was passed sanctioning legal distilling on payment of a duty of 2s. 3d. a gallon of proof spirit, and a licence fee of £10 for all stills with a capacity of forty gallons and over. This Act caused the good malt whisky to drive out the bad, but it meant that the duty had come to stay; and duties usually increase rather than otherwise. By 1914 the duty on whisky was 30s. a gallon. In 1920 it had risen to £3 12s. 6d. and remained at this figure till 1939. In the war it was increased several times and in 1941 the price was 16s. per bottle of which 11s. 4d. was tax. So the Scottish people have gradually been deprived of their natural drink. Sir Robert Bruce Lockhart has written:

> It says much for the patience and forbearance of the Scottish people that they have endured this deprivation without violent protest. It requires very little imagination to realize what would happen in France if ever a French Government tried to put wine beyond the reach of the French people.

And also:

> Most Scots – and I would say all Scots who think seriously of their country's future – are resolved that Scotland shall have a larger control of her own natural affairs, and of these whisky is certainly one.

I doubt if many islanders in 1941 had reasoned things out as coherently as this. But in all Scots there is a smouldering resentment that their drink should have been removed from them by a duty fixed in London. It is no use arguing that the Scots are a drunken race; even if they were – and I for one do not believe it – whisky still means much more to them than just a drink. It is a need, a symbol, a medicine, and their life's blood. Norman MacMillan said to me:

It is very difficult to explain, but there's one thing about it: if anything goes wrong it's the first thing you go and get and if you're celebrating you must have whisky; and even when every other medicine fails, you always fall back on whisky. It's something traditional that's always belonged to Scotland. You can't get it distilled or manufactured in any other place but Scotland. These Scots people, they're so strong . . . and it's the juice of the barley, I think, that keeps them so.

With these views so rooted in the whole community it is not surprising that there was a head-on clash with authority. Also, one must remember that these were not normal times; the war had been on for eighteen months and whisky (not to mention food and everything else) was short. The whole Hebrides were in a defence area and movement was restricted. The life of the islanders, hard at any time, was cribbed and confined. So if the law said they could not rescue the whisky, the law was an ass.

Never when I was on the islands did I ever hear the looting described as theft – always 'rescuing'. 'We rescued forty cases that night,' they would say. And Angus John:

Two months in prison – that's more than enough for rescuing some cases of whisky.

This euphemism may have been applied consciously, but I do not think so. In their own view it described exactly what they were doing. To Peter MacInnes, Norman MacMillan or Angus John, the idea of theft, taking from another individual, would be abhorrent. But who were they taking the whisky from? The owners, the salvors, or from whom? In their own view it was from the sea; and subsequent events were to prove this substantially correct. But what could have been done to resolve the situation, to stop the law taking its course and turning hitherto honest men into criminals, and sowing the seeds of bitterness for years to come? The Customs could have done no more, certainly. To begin with they had neither the men nor the equipment, but there was also the overriding point that the whisky was not theirs to dispose of. Their sole concern was that, if it were landed, then there should be no loss to the revenue. As Ivan Gledhill put it, 'If it did not come into consumption, then it was not our business.'

At this distance, the Customs' viewpoint may seem specialised to the point of absurdity, but the Customs were doing a very specialised job. But what of the salvors? It will be remembered that Commander Kay thought that the whisky was not worth bothering about. This statement is hard to take at its face value. In 1941 (as already mentioned) the retail price was 16s. a bottle, so even at that rate the whisky was worth £211,000. Also, in the same hold, as I was to discover later on, there was cargo worth even more than that. One cannot escape the conclusion that Kay was under specific orders to salvage whatever he could quickly and easily, and to leave everything else, no matter what the value. This is confirmed by the Liverpool and Glasgow Salvage Association official who said, 'We were dealing with up to five wrecks a day – we needed the equipment.' But the fact remains that Kay and his ships, divers and equipment were with the *Politician* for over a month. Could not the whisky have been dealt with in this time?

David Shaw thinks that with a little imagination and foresight, it could have been. He said:

> Why did not the salvage people say to McColl: 'Recruit local fishermen – as many as you want – to clear the wreck. Give them a bottle or so each in payment.' It would have saved endless trouble to the salvors, the Customs, the police, and the courts.

One cannot help thinking that the Procurator-Fiscal is right.

There is evidence too that the law officers at the time, both locally and in the Lord Advocate's Department, felt that things had been bungled. As already noted, the looters were let off on technicalities even if caught red-handed; and the maximum penalty for theft (three months) was never awarded even to the worst cases. From the Customs documents it is evident that Gledhill, quite reasonably from his viewpoint, wanted the worst offenders to be made an example of and charged under the Customs Act. But this was not done. In fact I am told that the Procurator-Fiscal had promised to advise the Customs when the charges of theft were to be heard so that the Customs could bring their more serious charges at the same time. But the Customs were not so advised and their opportunity was lost. This may have been a mistake or a misunderstanding; but it looks much more like a deliberate policy. Many people who were caught with stolen property in their crofts were never charged at all; and no one was charged after the mass raid on Eriskay, although a hundred or more cases of whisky, not to mention other things, were confiscated. Altogether, one receives the impression that the authorities were worried by the temper of the islanders. They knew that by enforcing the law, they were bringing it into disrepute. By May, when the shipbreakers arrived, the situation had become so bad that something had to be done to put an end to the tragi-comedy of the *Politician*, for that is what it had now become. So in June, about the time that the bulk of the men sent to prison were beginning their sentence, there was perpetrated what many believe to be the greatest outrage in the long and turbulent history of Scotland; an outrage so great that even today, over twenty years later, strong men are liable to quiver at the very mention of it; an outrage which proved to the islanders, conclusively and for all time, that the authorities had gone out of their minds, and that they themselves were the last stronghold of sanity in a crazy world.

CHAPTER 7

The Days of the Shipbreakers

WHEN P E HOLDEN, Duncan McIver and their fifteen men arrived on 12 May, the *Politician* presented a sorry spectacle. The hull had begun to rust, the decks were filthy and covered with oil, clay and salt, while down below the air was acrid with the stink of fuel oil. All the cabins had been looted and their fixtures torn out, and even some pianos on board had been senselessly smashed.

Examination by the divers showed that there was a great rock under the engine-room, and the bulkhead had been pushed right up so that No. 5 hold, the engine-room, and the stokehole had become one great tank, the water flowing from one compartment to the other.

Under Holden's instructions, the propeller and its broken shaft were brought up on to the deck, and to his surprise he found that the former was undamaged. He could not understand why this should be, as the rudder was smashed, and he wondered if the accident had been caused by the rudder striking a rock and thereby throwing the ship off course. As I was able to explain to him when we met at Stirling, the rudder was damaged by the gales on 15 February, the divers reporting that 'the rudder post is bent to 45 degrees.' Holden, of course, like everyone else who saw the ship, was amazed at its rock-bound situation. As he said, if he had not seen for himself he would never have believed it.

The first job was to lighten her; and to this end he ordered his men to go down and remove what cargo was left in the for'ard holds, while the divers dealt with the more inaccessible bales of cloth and cases of whisky below the water-line in No. 5 hold. His main effort now was to start removing all the superstructure;

and gradually the *Politician* ceased to look like a ship and acquired the forlorn appearance of a hulk. In a few months, everything above deck level had disappeared, and even the upper decks themselves. Meanwhile the divers were down below plugging up the holes in the ship's skin with plates, which all had to be riveted. The purpose of this operation was to render as many compartment of the ship as possible watertight, and then airtight. Once this had been achieved, air could be pumped in under pressure, and, given suitable conditions including a high tide, the *Politician* could then be floated off without difficulty.

As might be expected, the operation was long and tedious. To begin with, there was the size of the damage to the outer skin, the fracture near the main injection extending to fourteen feet; and all compartments aft of No. 2 hold were fractured to some extent. Also, in rough water or when the currents were too strong, the work could not proceed at all, and in this way hours or even days were lost. It was towards the end of August, that is almost four months after Holden's arrival, before an attempt to float the ship off could even be contemplated, and by this time the divers and the rest of the men were sorry they had ever heard the name *Politician*. Apart from the rigours of the work, they had to live on Eriskay, a beautiful island for anyone making a home there by choice, but bereft of all modern amenities, even a public house. The charm of the scenery, if it had ever existed for them, had long palled, and all they had to look forward to was an occasional trip home. What they said about the captain who had wrecked his ship in such a place is fortunately not recorded.

To anyone unfamiliar with the business of shipbreaking and salvage, it may seem doubtful whether this great effort in terms of men, equipment, and time, was worthwhile. Why, it might be argued, could not the ship be cut up where she lay, and taken to the mainland piece by piece, as was the superstructure? The answer is that Messrs Arnott, Young and Company wanted every single scrap of steel they could get their hands on, not just the hull above the water-line, but right down to the keel. Also, with their equipment at Rothesay, they could cut up the ship much more quickly and effectively than they could *in situ*. It is possible, of course, that had they appreciated from the beginning the *Politician*'s extraordinary reluctance to die, they might have changed their plans. But, as it was, they had Holden's word that he could float her off; and the only thing to do was to wait.

From the early days after the wreck, there had been persistent rumours that there was a vast quantity of money aboard the *Politician*. Whether this rumour was originated by the Purser or one of the officers it is now impossible to say, but when the looting was at its height many of the islanders spent some of their time poking around for the strong-room, though without success. When I was up in the islands I came across vague rumours about the money, but no one would admit to having seen any, let alone having handled it. Whether this was merely caution, or the islanders were telling the truth, I could not judge at the time. But, having a curious belief in rumours, even the wildest of them, I persisted in my attempts to unearth the truth. My resolution was perhaps strengthened by the fact that stories about the money had been circulating in London, apart from the Hebrides, and I even met people who swore they had seen newspaper articles on the subject. I was never able to track down these articles either then or since, but they may well have existed, as the London rumours turned out to be substantially correct.

The first clue I stumbled on was a remark made by David Shaw, the Procurator-Fiscal, on the last day of my visit to the Hebrides. We had been going through the Register of Charges for an hour or more, when he suddenly looked up and asked, 'Did you know there was some money aboard the *Polly*?'

'I've never been able to prove it,' I said.

'It's a curious thing,' he replied, 'but one afternoon when I was out with Neil Campbell in his boat, he said: 'I've handled something I bet you've never seen – money from the *Polly*'.'

'What sort of money?'

'He wouldn't say then – and I've never been able to drag it out of him.'

'Do you think he's pulling your leg?'

'No – I'm sure he wasn't. Many people have told me there was money aboard – but Neil's the only one claiming to have handled it.'

As Neil Campbell had obviously not wished to talk to me, and I could not get back to Ludag in any case, there was no alternative to letting the matter drop for the moment. In fact, I did not pick up the next clue till I visited Ivan Gledhill.

'Money?' he said to me, in reply to a question. 'Yes, there was some on board – but not sterling.'

'What was it then?'

'Chinese currency. While I was up there, the salvors turned up five boxes, all packed with notes. I've got one of them here.' He showed it to me, stuck in his album among the photographs. 'Curiously enough,' he added, 'I received a report from McColl, some time afterwards, that a sixth box had been washed up on the shores of South Uist. But all the money from it had vanished.'

At the time I thought this must be the money Neil Campbell had referred to, though a lingering doubt persisted in my mind, possibly because the rumours in London had mentioned sterling. As Holden had been the last man aboard the *Politician*, I made a note to probe him on the subject, but when we eventually met there was so much to talk about that he was already picking up his hat before I remembered. Hearing my question, however, he swung round in surprise, saying: 'How on earth did you know about the money?' When I told him Gledhill's story his surprise increased. 'I never heard about that,' he said. 'The stuff we found was all ten-shilling notes.'

Somewhat excited, I pressed for further details, to be met at first with a curious reluctance. However, to my relief, he did eventually open up.

The salvors had told me [he said] there was some money aboard, but they didn't know in what form or how much, and I rather came to the conclusion that they were pulling my leg. However, I started searching for the strong-room and eventually found it hidden between decks in the No. 5 hold. It was locked, so I got my men on to it and we pulled it apart. It took us some time, I can tell you. Once in there we opened the safe – but all we found were a few cheques and papers, none of them very interesting. So I came to the conclusion that the salvors didn't know what they were talking about – they'd just been sold on wild rumours. Anyhow I couldn't spend any more time searching. We were still trying to make the various compartments airtight, and that was a big enough job in itself. Then one morning – it was my day off – I thought I'd have a trip to Eriskay and forget all about the ship for a few hours. Try and get the foul stink of fuel oil out of my nostrils. It was all very quiet and peaceful. . . and I was walking along the sand when I happened to see some children – three girls and a boy – playing shops. As I was not in any hurry, I turned to look at them, and then, to my surprise, I realized that they were playing with bundles of real notes! They were ten shillings, for issue in Jamaica. I asked the children where they'd got them from and they told me, 'We picked them up on the beach.' 'How did they get there?' I asked. 'They come in on the sea,' they told me. 'They're coming in all the time.' Not exactly believing them, I walked along the shore to have a look myself and after a bit I found one. It was a ten-shilling Jamaican note, almost torn in half. I knew there was money aboard now!

Next day I got the divers together and started the search. Most of the holds were pretty well empty now – only No. 5 hold had much stuff in it, so we started there. There was a whole mountain of stuff to move, great bales of cloth, not to mention the whisky that was still left, but eventually we found something – a tin box crammed with notes. It must have been right in the middle of the whisky cases. We went on till we found a couple more boxes. They were full of ten-shilling Jamaican notes too. I counted it and it came to £360,000.

I took the notes out and packed them into tin boxes, then I went across to Lochboisdale to post them off to Arnott, Young and Company. I'd wrapped them up and sealed them with my own ring – with an H. The Postmistress asked me what was the contents of the boxes and when I replied, '£360,000 in cash', she nearly did a back somersault. Then she weighed the boxes and complained that they were over-weight. However, she took them in the end, and eventually Arnott, Young handed them over to the Bank of England.

'Did you get any reward?' I asked.

'No – the Bank of England sent me a letter of thanks, but that was all.'

He told me two other stories about the money. When he was in Rothesay – in the autumn of 1941 – an RAF corporal who had tried to change some Jamaican notes was reported to the police and charged with stealing them from the *Politician*. Luckily, however, he was able to prove that he had been serving in the West

Indies and had brought the money home with him on leave. The other story was that a large quantity of notes had been handed into Messrs Thomas Cook only a few years ago. Though he could not say how this had originated, he had a theory that one of the salvors had got hold of a box and helped himself without telling anyone.

Back in London, I wrote to Messrs Cooks, who referred me to the Crown Agents for Overseas Governments and Administrations. From them I learned that soon after the *Politician* ran aground reports began to come in from the Scottish police that Jamaican notes were circulating in the Hebrides, as far north as Benbecula, and efforts were made to get them in. After a time, quite considerable quantities were, in fact, recovered and destroyed. But even more must have found their way across the Minch, for from 1947 to 1957 they kept on being presented for exchange at Cooks offices in various parts of the country. The quantities were apparently so large that the authorities began extensive inquiries, but by that time the notes had passed through several hands and it was thought that the bulk of them had been presented in good faith. The source from which they had been filtered into circulation during these eleven years was never located – or at least, if it was, no prosecution ensued. Since December, 1958, no further notes from the *Politician* have appeared; but according to the Crown Agents, 'large numbers of notes are still unaccounted for'. It is very probable that the bulk of them have long since rotted on the sea-bed off Eriskay, or have been swept out into the Atlantic. But, personally, I suspect that somewhere in Scotland or England there is a gentleman sitting on a great stack of them, unable to bring himself to shovel them into the fire, yet not daring to exchange them, for fear of prosecution. Perhaps when he dies we shall learn who he is, and how he came to get hold of the notes.

So that is the story of the money aboard the *Politician*. The extraordinary thing is that its existence was not known from the start. As will be remembered, Gledhill sent to Liverpool for the outward file of the ship as soon as he learned of the accident. Obviously this could not have contained any mention of the money, or he would have known about it immediately. As it was, he only stumbled across the Chinese currency by accident, and when I saw him he still had no idea that there had been Jamaican currency aboard. If it is not the custom to mention currency carried for overseas on cargo manifests, then one would have expected the owners or whoever was dispatching the currency to advise the salvors. Or, right at the beginning, why did not Captain Worthington advise Commander Kay? Why should so much time have been spent salvaging bicycles and spare parts while the currency was left? And finally: why was the currency stored down among bales of cloth and cases of whisky? The whole episode is very curious.

Early in September, Holden was ready for his attempt to float the *Politician* off the rocks. From the tide-table the most favourable day appeared to be the 22nd, and he laid his plans carefully for that date. The final tests were carried out, the pumping gear was assembled, and all he needed was some fine weather. Fortunately, as the locals had predicted, it was excellent, and they thought it would hold. If they were right, then the prospects of success were good because only on a perfectly calm day could the job be done. For the next four days the pumping went on almost day and night; Holden, McIver and his men working themselves almost to the point of exhaustion. The climax to four months' hard work was at hand. If the *Politician* came off, not only would this work be vindicated, but the men could escape from the Hebrides. So, anxiously, they watched the ship rise out of the water inch by inch as the air pressure increased.

The fact that its hull was filthy with rust and covered with barnacles did not worry them – all they cared about was that she should rise. For the great occasion Gledhill was on board with McColl, both of them no doubt earnestly praying that the ship, or what was left of it, would be taken out of their territory for ever. Also present were the Superintendent Salvage Engineer of the Iron and Steel (Salvage) Corporation, and a Captain Lauretson of the Ministry of Supply. At a distance, some in boats and even more on the shores, were the men of Eriskay and South Uist. They would be sad to see the last of the *Politician*; she had brought trouble and bitterness, but she had also brought the most wonderful cargo ever to be landed in the Hebrides. She was the most famous ship in all their history.

When I was up there, the floating of the *Politician* was already a legend. Norman MacMillan said to me:

> It was a good salvage job. They pumped her full of compressed air and they judged the tide – in fact, they misjudged the tide. At a certain hour the tugs got at her and they tried to pull her off, but she wouldn't budge. Two or three times they tried and gave it up and went away. Then someone looked behind, and all of a sudden the poor old *Politician* was swinging off by herself. Those few extra inches of water and she was just swinging off the rock.

That is the legend – which is true and yet untrue. Holden did not misjudge the tide; what happened was that it came in an hour late. To anyone accustomed to the regular time-tables of Margate or Brighton, this may seem incredible. But in that complex pattern of land and water, and the web of currents around the Hebrides, tides can vary. It is rare on a calm day like this that a tide should be a full hour late, but on 22 September, 1941, it did happen, for Gledhill's account of events was confirmed later by

Holden. It must have been a very anxious time. Every pound of air had been pumped into the ship; nothing more could be done, and if the tide did not reach its full height the chance of floating the ship might be lost. There was only a week left of September and with October would come the gales. It was definitely a case of now or never.

Holden, Lauretson, Gledhill, McColl and the Superintendent Engineer were all standing on the deck, anxiously watching the water level, when suddenly there was a shout. It came from Duncan McIver who, black with oil from head to foot, was running towards them along the deck.

'She's afloat!' he cried. 'The bloody thing's afloat!'

To his relief Holden saw that this was a fact. Gently pulled by the *Assistance*, the old wreck had slid straight off the rock which had gripped her since that dark night in February, and was moving slowly but on an even keel towards the centre of the Sound. A loud cheer went up from the men at the pumps, and Holden smiled a smile of relief. He had told his Company that he would get her off, and now, though it had cost him and his men seventeen weeks of hard labour, he had done it.

As he well knew, the ship could not be towed to Rothesay or the Clyde by the *Assistance*; the job would require heavy tugs which could only be obtained after due notice had been given. His plan, therefore, was to tow her round to Lochboisdale and beach her there till the tugs could arrive. The journey he estimated – some seven or eight miles – could be accomplished in under three hours, and he was confident that he could keep the ship afloat for that time. The local prophets assured him that the weather would hold, and the sea was as calm as it was ever likely to be. He therefore proposed that the journey should begin at once, and Lauretson agreed with him. But, to his surprise and horror, the Superintendent Engineer of the Iron and Steel

Corporation began raising objections. In his view, he said, the risk was too great; for if they ran into rough weather in the Minch, or the compressed air compartments failed to hold, the ship would go down into deep water and would be irrecoverable.

Holden (still supported by Lauretson) fought this argument. He staked his professional reputation on the compartments holding – and pointed out that there was no rough water in the Minch at the moment. Furthermore, he said, they had only just got the ship afloat after tremendous effort – and the logical, sensible course was to keep her afloat. The argument (Gledhill told me) went on for some hours, while the ship drifted north towards South Uist. But the Superintendent Engineer would not budge; he was scared stiff of risking the Minch, and as he came from the contractors, Arnott, Young being the sub-contractors, his decision had to be accepted. Under Holden's orders, the ship was pulled west to a point some five hundred yards north of Calvay where there was a sandbank. Here the pressure valves were released, the air hissed out of the sealed compartments and for the second time the *Politician* sank down on to the bottom. But what Holden did not know, what no one knew, was that in the centre of the sandbank a rock was concealed. And the *Politician* broke her back on it.

At first this disaster was not apparent. Later on the 22nd a confident signal was sent off by the Superintendent Engineer to his employers via the Salvage Association.

> Steamer *Politician* has re-floated and been safely berthed at Eriskay.

Even a week later, he was still not disillusioned:

> 30 September. Arrangements are being made to beach steamer
> *Politician* in Lochboisdale. Vessel will be ready for towage on 3
> October.

On 25 October, tugs were dispatched to take the *Politician* from Eriskay to Lochboisdale, but despite all their pumping operations she would not rise off the bottom. The Superintendent Engineer blamed the tide; but further examination by the divers confirmed Holden's worst fears. She would never rise now – at least not in one piece. So the tugs were sent away again and Holden must have watched them disappear up the Minch with a sense of frustration and bitterness.

On 1 December yet another expert appeared in the person of the Salvage Association Surveyor. Once more the battered hulk was examined, and the same day the Surveyor signalled:

> Steamer *Politician* has sustained further serious damage as the
> result of pounding and striking bottom during recent gales.
> Concur with salvor's view that all operations be suspended
> until April next and for'ard section then be cut off and towed
> away for breaking up. This is best hoped for; at worst vessel to
> be broken up *in situ*.

So the tragi-comic story of the *Politician* went on. The Hebrides showed no sign of relaxing their grip on her, and everything conspired to help them. . . the timidity of the Superintendent Engineer, the rock in the sandbank, the failure of the tide, and now the approach of winter. Holden could be forgiven for deciding that fate and the elements had ganged up against him and that for the moment anyway further struggling was useless.

In June, Gledhill had mooted that the only way to solve the Customs problem, if the remainder of the whisky could not be removed, was to destroy it. He therefore asked Holden if it would be possible to put some dynamite charges in No. 5 hold; but Holden was still in the middle of his efforts to get the ship afloat and did not want to risk damaging its frail skin with dynamite. Pleading technical reasons, he declined Gledhill's suggestion; but in October, with the ship's back broken on the sandbank, the situation was quite different, and when Gledhill approached him again he knew there was no valid reason for refusing. Reckoning that there were a thousand cases in the hold, he estimated that six charges should be enough, so he had them brought over from the mainland, put them down in the hold at low tide and detonated them. Twelve thousand bottles of whisky (or so it was hoped) were destroyed in a flash. They would never, to use the Customs phrase, 'come into consumption'. There would be no further loss to the revenue. As far as Gledhill and McColl were concerned, the nightmare was over.

With the effective intelligence services at their disposal, the islanders had heard all about the arrival of the dynamite charges, and so, when the explosion reverberated across the Sound, they knew just what had happened. The actual loss of the whisky did not upset them so much, as the Customs search was virtually over and they still had ample stocks in hand. But the fact that anyone should resort to dynamite, rather than concentrate their efforts to rescue the whisky, quite outraged them. It was the ultimate in stupidity, waste, and vandalism, symbolizing a mental attitude quite beyond their comprehension. They knew now, if they had not done before, that they had been right to carry out their 'rescue' operation; for if they had not done so, thousands of cases, Highland Glen, Stag's Head, and Haig, would have been blown sky-high with the thousand cases that were left.

'Dynamiting whisky!' Angus John said to me. 'You wouldn't think there'd be men in the world so crazy as *that*!'

All that winter the *Politician* lay on the bottom of the Sound of Eriskay; and it was not until March, 1942, that Holden and his crew returned. With them they brought underwater acetylene cutters, and began the job of severing the No. 5 hold and the stern from the for'ard sections of the ship. The job was long and difficult, and from time to time was hindered by rough water or strong currents. The divers were scared of getting pinned between the two sections as, half cut away, these swung in the tide; and they had frequently to come up to rest. Also, there was the business of the acetylene gas. This had to be brought across from Glasgow in great containers, trans-shipped to the *Assistance* and then transported carefully up the shallow waters of the Sound. If anything went wrong with these administrative arrangements, work immediately came to a full stop. Altogether, operations went on for the best part of a month; but in the end they were successful. Freed of the burden of the waterlogged No. 5 hold, the ship came off the bottom without further trouble, and on a calm spring day Holden (having patched her up again and pumped in air) was able to tow her round to Lochboisdale. Here she waited till the tugs arrived to take her across the Minch to Rothesay; and this time there was no mistake. Within a fortnight, the ship – or what was left of her – made a pathetic entry into the shipbreakers' yard, where she was cut up into sections without ceremony.

Meanwhile the No. 5 hold remained where it lay, and, sinking a few inches deeper into the sand each year, it remains there still. Sometimes it almost seems as if the islands were determined that this section of the ship at least, the section which yielded such an extraordinary harvest, should stay with them for ever.

CHAPTER 8

The Mystery Explored

THE GREATEST MYSTERY of the whole *Politician* story is, of course, how did she come to be wrecked there in the first place? Why was she sailing full steam ahead up a shallow rock-bound channel? Why was her head pointing north west instead of north east? This has generally been regarded as one of the most tantalizing sea mysteries in recent years. As Alasdair Alpin McGregor puts it:

> How any ship of her size, under control, as one presumes the *Politician* to have been, came to grief at this spot, even under the black-out conditions of wartime then prevailing, is a mystery.

The islanders have a simple solution. 'It was the islanders calling her,' they say; or 'It was the islands calling the whisky.' Others, less fanciful, say, 'It was the cargo that put her off course' – implying that the crew had got some of it inside them. This explanation, in fact, has been widely (and erroneously) accepted, and not only in the islands. Ivan Gledhill said to me: 'They were drunk – they must have been.' Sir Compton Mackenzie (who was living on Barra at the time) said to me when I saw him at his home in Edinburgh: 'If they weren't drunk, I cannot think of any other explanation.'

Anxious to track down the sources of these stories, I questioned one of the first outsiders to make contact with the crew – Allan MacDonald, the mechanic on the Barra lifeboat, who has already been mentioned. To the question, 'Did anyone tell you there was whisky on board?' he replied, 'We could see there was plenty of whisky on board, as many of the crew had bottles sticking out of their pockets.' And later he said, 'All the crew seemed to be very happy, as I think they had a good share of the cargo of whisky.'

To the question, 'What was your impression of the Captain?' he replied, 'I would not say he was sober. He looked a little dazed.'

There can be no doubt, in my view, that it was largely from these impressions of the lifeboat crew that the stories of drunkenness originated, stimulated of course by the lack of any other reasonable explanation. But (as I began to ask myself) was this the truth, or the whole truth? If the Captain was drunk, was he on the bridge at the time? If not, who was? and was *he* drunk? The crime of wrecking a great ship through incapacity owing to alcohol would, of course, be a frightful one; but, as one must acknowledge, drunken captains have been known and accidents at sea have been caused, though not frequently, in the most disreputable manner. The only thing to do was to assemble all the evidence available and to examine it dispassionately.

The first point about MacDonald's evidence is, of course, that when he arrived at 4 pm the accident was already over eight hours old. Therefore, whatever the condition of the Captain and the crew when he saw them, it need not necessarily have any relation to their condition at 7.45 am. Furthermore half the crew had been hanging around all day, not knowing what was happening, and with little to do; if they had sunk a few drams while they waited, it would not be surprising. Worthington even, in the worry and stress, may have hit the bottle, but this still would not have been a fact relevant to the accident. Fortunately, however, I was able to track down evidence from other sources.

As may be recalled, through the assistance of the Mercantile Marine Association I was able to establish that both Worthington and Baker, the Second Officer, were dead. But from Fothergill Cottrell and Huntington I had learned that the officer on the bridge at the time of the accident was R A Swain, the Mate. On my visit to Liverpool to see the Secretary of the Association, I made inquiries about Swain, but at first no record of him could be found. Then it was discovered that the clerk was looking for a member called 'Swayne', and once the error had been pointed out he soon found the right dossier. Swain's address was there, and various details of his service, but at the end there was a brief note in red. He had died in February, 1962, just two months previously. I wrote to his widow, but unfortunately she had no papers or any information about the incident at all.

This left (of the deck officers) only Reuben Platt, who had last been heard of in Preston. After several attempts, I was able to track him down, helped by a free-lance journalist; but all Platt would say was that the accident happened a long time ago and he could remember very little about it. Further attempts to encourage him to refresh his memory have failed completely. But (and I quote Huntington here) Platt had gone off watch at midnight, that is nearly eight hours before the accident, and anything he learned would have been from Worthington or Swain. And, as we already know, they were never able to give a coherent explanation of the accident, either then or later.

But to return to the drunkenness charge. Both Huntington and Cottrell assert that this is without foundation so far as the men on the bridge were concerned. On the other hand it is very probable, indeed almost indisputable, that some of the crew had got at the cargo. Cottrell says that there was a bottom way into No. 5 hold via the base of the mast; and if there is a way to Scotch, some men will always find it. But as regards Swain their evidence must, I think, be accepted. They both saw him soon after the accident – Cottrell within minutes of it – and their memories seem quite clear on this point. Cottrell too wrote a long account of the adventure when he reached home a week or so later and, as might be expected, every detail was sharp in his mind. He was only seventeen years of age, and this was, after all, his first voyage. But what about Worthington? According to Huntington, he was quite a heavy drinker, though no one serving under him ever suggested that he let his drinking interfere with the job. The curious thing, though, is that he should have been in bed at the time. According to Cottrell (who served on with the line for some years) there was a company rule that in coastal waters the Captain should remain on the bridge. Why should he have disregarded the rule so flagrantly? Cottrell suggests that his knowledge and trust of Swain were so great that he felt his presence on the bridge was quite unnecessary. When Cottrell arrived there, a few minutes after the accident, he was still half dressed, having slipped his trousers on over his pyjamas, and was ordering 'Full ahead' and 'Full astern' in a desperate effort to free the ship. As must have been only too clear to him, his disobedience to the company rule had brought disaster; but, unless it is suggested that he was toping in bed, the incident does absolve him of any charge of drunkenness. Cottrell's view is that he had just been awakened from a deep sleep, his eyes not yet being fully open. Huntington supports this.

But how does all this square with the reports of the lifeboat crew? The overriding fact is surely the one already dealt with: that they arrived a good eight hours later on. We need not doubt that the statement that Worthington was dazed is correct; but surely his experiences, since he was rudely awakened by the accident, would have been enough to daze anyone. It should be remembered too that just before the arrival of the lifeboat the mist had lifted, showing the extraordinary position his ship had got herself into. One can visualize him on the deck gazing at South Uist to starboard, Eriskay to port, Calvay straight ahead, and Hartamul astern, and between them the rocks jutting out of the sea. 'How the hell,' he must have asked himself, 'am I going to explain this to the company?' Moreover it is very probable that, until the lifeboat coxswain told him his true position, he still imagined himself to be south of Barra.

Where was the ship trying to go? In 1941 all shipping was routed by the Admiralty and the Ministry of War Transport, and the *Politician's* precise orders would seem to be lost or at least buried until such time as they turn up in the Public Record Office, towards the end of the century. Owing to wartime security, it is probable that they were only known by Worthington and Swain; certainly Huntington and Cottrell have no information about them. From the evidence in the possession of HM Customs there would seem to be no doubt that she was steaming north towards Loch Ewe, where she was to rendezvous with a convoy for Jamaica and the United States. She would not have been allowed to cross the Atlantic alone, and according to Cottrell the crew had to be informed whether the voyage would be in convoy, or they would not sign on. But which route was she taking to her RV? Up the Minch (that is between the mainland and the Outer Hebrides), or round the west of the Hebrides? It has been suggested that the reason for the accident was that she was trying to cross to the west of the islands (that is taking the second route). Sir Compton Mackenzie said to me: 'I always understood that she took the wrong turning.' This opinion would seem to be reinforced by the fact that her head was pointing north west; and also by the SOS signals which gave her position as south of Barra. But against it, there is a statement from MacDonald that when the lifeboatmen asked the officers where they were trying to go, they said 'Up the Minch.' This, of course, is not conclusive (even taken with the information from HM Customs) and for a while I had a strong feeling that it was mis-taken. Later, however, I was able to obtain further evidence from MacDonald which in my view is conclusive. This was that about six miles to the south of the accident, about eighteen minutes previously, the ship had been steaming on a course of 015 degrees to 020 degrees.

The incident which furnished the proof was that she cut the under-sea cable between Barra and South Uist, at a point four miles south west of Eriskay – that is, off the island of Flodday. From the Scottish headquarters of the GPO I obtained a map showing the lie of the cable in 1941. In sending it, the engineers explained that one cannot guarantee the position of cables to a foot or two as they can be moved by currents and under-water disturbances, but with this qualification the map was accurate. From it, one can see quite clearly that from this point to the north east corner of Eriskay a course of 015 degrees would have been necessary; but, by the nature of the coast, it is quite inconceivable that the ship could have sailed close inshore all the way up, and a course of 020 degrees or even 025 degrees seems much more likely. She could not have been steaming on this course if Worthington contemplated going up to the west of the Hebrides.

The solution of this, the first problem, however, leads to two further questions:

(a) Why should she be so far over to the west?
(b) Why, if she were on a course of 015 degrees or 020 degrees at 7.28 am, should she have altered through 60 degrees by 7.45 am?

Let us take (a) first. The accepted track up the Minch, according to the West Coast of Scotland Pilot and the charts, lies about sixteen miles to the east of the point where the *Politician* cut the cable; the down track is about eight miles nearer. It is very doubtful – and I have the word of several sailors for this – that the Admiralty would have directed her up the Minch on the downward track, or a track which involved her going close to these treacherous coastlines. In wartime, with no side-lights, lighthouses dimmed, and buoys unlit, this would have been to invite disaster. Accepting this, it is apparent that the ship was sixteen miles off her proper track. How had it happened?

The first thing which springs to mind, of course, is the compass. In 1941, gyro-compasses were not so common as they are today, and the *Politician* was equipped solely with a magnetic compass. These instruments, as all sailors know, have to be guarded very carefully, for not only are they affected by any alterations to the ship – and in wartime the degaussing gear or the protective plating was always being seen to between voyages – but also by the cargo, especially if it contains any appreciable quantity of metal. The *Politician*'s cargo (as we know) included cars and a large stock of bicycles and spare parts, so one would have expected the Captain, on leaving port, to have carried out the usual drill of swinging the ship – that is, turning her through 360 degrees to ascertain the compass variation on each bearing. (The variation or error need not be uniform; it could be, for example, one degree when the ship's head is pointing north, and three when it is pointing west.) There is no record in the log, however, that Worthington did swing the ship, and Cottrell has no recollection of it being done. If there was a compass error – and I am not stating at this stage that there was – it may well have taken the ship over to the west. One must remember that even before she was through the North Channel the night had closed in and the sky was covered with cloud. Neither the stars nor the moon were visible for an observation, so the ship was sailing by dead reckoning. An error of 10 degrees at a point opposite the Skerryvore would have taken her sixteen miles off track by the time she came up to Eriskay. Ten degrees, of course, though not impossible, is a very great error; but even if it existed it still could not account for events which happened subsequently. There is another point to consider. As the *Politician* was steaming on a course of roughly 015 degrees when she hit the cable, she must, earlier on, have been even farther to the west. If Huntington is right in his belief that during his watch, from 4 am onwards, there was no violent change of course, she may even have been south west of Barra Head.

How did she get there? Allowing for a possible compass error, it would seem quite certain that it was the convoy which threw her off course. She met this in the dark, to the north of Ireland, and for half an hour or more threaded her way through it. With dimmed side-lights, on a choppy sea, and with half a gale blowing from the south east, this must have been no easy piece of pilotage, to say the least; and the result of it may have been to draw the *Politician* some miles to the west. Cottrell, who watched the operation, is definitely of this opinion. There is also the possibility, though I would not put it stronger than that, that the tidal stream may have edged her to the west. According to the West Coast of Scotland Pilot, in the approaches to the Sea of the Hebrides it is clockwise in motion and increases in strength towards the shores. The *Politician*, therefore, already too far west, may have become subject to the stream, which at the southern end of its movement would have been travelling from east to west.

So, for the sake of argument, let us assume that:

(a) The necessity of threading its way through the convoy took the *Politician* off course to the west.
(b) A compass error took her farther across.
(c) The tidal stream aggravated the error.

The point to consider now is: Why, at 7.28 am, was she steaming on a course of 015 degrees to 020 degrees? The normal track up through the Minch involves – in the earlier stages – a course between due north and 005 degrees. If the ship had been in her correct position her course would therefore have taken her slap into the Skerryvore, or, if she happened to miss that, into Tiree or Coll. From this it seems likely that Worthington may have realized that he was too far to the west and set a course to correct the position. But here his error regarding latitude came into play, the ship being twenty miles farther north than he imagined. The course of 015 degrees (if he had held to it) would still have brought him against the shores of South Uist. In fact, the ship needed to be at least two miles farther to the east to clear the island, steaming on this course. If she had cleared it, however, she could have gone straight up the Minch, on an erratic course, admittedly, but well clear of land.

That, however, is pure speculation, the facts being that she was fatally far west – and she ran aground. But the curious thing is that she did not continue on her course and come to grief where one would have expected: in the area of Rudha Dubh on South Uist. Somehow or other she turned in an arc of 60 degrees towards the west, all in a matter of eighteen minutes. If the islands were calling the whisky, they were certainly making their voices felt!

Why this change of course? Had Worthington ordered it? Or did Swain, on his own initiative? And for what reason? Surely they did not imagine that they were dangerously close to the Skerryvore, to the east. Huntington's recollection is that there was no sudden change of course' and with his long experience of the sea he must have noticed some change in motion. Also, it must be remembered that there was no change in speed; she had been going steadily at full steam ahead for some hours. It may be argued, of course, that her head swung round at the moment of impact, or as she rode over the rock, before it finally pierced her outer skin and crashed through into the engine-room. But both Cottrell and Huntington believe that she rode straight over the rock; and their view would seem to be confirmed by the divers' report, already quoted:

> 60 feet of keel aft with shell plating up to shaft open and fractured.

She may have swung a few degrees, but there would seem to be no possibility that she swung violently.

Did she swing to the west *after* the accident? At first sight, and bearing in mind the powerful currents in the Minch and up the Sound of Eriskay, this would seem to be a possibility. But it is absolutely denied by Holden who surely knew more about this matter than anyone. He said to me: 'She could not have moved. The rocks held her like a vice.' The photographs taken at various dates confirm this.

If the above is correct, as I believe, the ship must have swung during the eighteen minutes before the accident. Why should this have happened? The first clue I picked up was a statement by Allan MacDonald, who told me: 'Eriskay is famous for wrecks, owing to a hill there which is supposed to interfere with ships' compasses.' If this were true, then the legends, the half-joking assertions of the islanders were right after all. *The islands were calling the whisky!* But what was the scientific or other evidence to support MacDonald's belief?

He was certainly right when he said that Eriskay was famous for shipwrecks. Within a few hundred yards of Calvay, eight or nine ships have run aground. One of them, the *Thala*, hit the rocks of Hartamul only four days after the *Politician* had come to grief. In 1940 a 4,000-ton ship, the *Birchol*, had ran aground there, and before the war a larger ship called the *Ayrshire*. The islanders also told me about a ship towing a floating dock which hit the coast of South Uist, just beyond Calvay, and John McIsaac, when I was out with him in his boat, showed me the exact spot. But all these accidents seemed to happen up to, or in the early years of the war; no one has been able to tell me of one since 1942. This may be, of course, because not so many ships are using the Minch, or other reasons; but it may also be because most ships have since acquired gyro-compasses – for which the song of the islands is sung in vain.

As I was unable to obtain information locally, Eriskay being something of a secret kingdom, I wrote to the Royal Geographical Society and the Geological Survey (a Government unit engaged in surveying the whole country). The former, though suggesting various lines of investigation, was unable to help, but Mr T M R Lawrie of the Edinburgh office of the Geological Survey was very enlightening. He informed me that the survey had not yet reached the Outer Hebrides, but that two scientists, the late Professor John and Dr Craig, had done a private survey which had been published by the Royal Society of Edinburgh in 1925. I contacted the Society, to be told, however, that Dr Craig was dead. Also, on Lawrie's advice, I contacted Doctor W Bullerwell, the Chief Geophysicist of the Geological Survey in London. In a long informative letter, he explained to me that no detailed magnetic surveys had been made in the area of the Outer Hebrides where the *Politician* ran aground. The most recent survey was published in 1896 by Rucker and Thorpe, and covered points in Barra and South Uist, but none of them nearer than ten miles to Eriskay. The Doctor continued:

You will see that though many of these (magnetic) deviations are quite large as compared with quieter areas elsewhere (for example, south east England) the maximum deviation between stations does not exceed Three degrees. But it is not possible to make any certain predictions about the likely deviations in the sea area on the basis of land measurements. The problem really comes down to predicting local sub-marine geology in an area of very complicated structure.

It would seem therefore that so far as Eriskay and the possibility of a lode hill is concerned there is no certain information. However, from a geological point of view, Lawrie has this to say:

> Magnetite is a common minor constituent of many rock types but it is only where it is present in comparatively large concentrations that the rock becomes noticeably magnetic. The gabbroic rocks which occur in the Cuillin Hills of Skye, in Rum, and in West Ardnamurchan are noticeably magnetic, as are some of the granitic gneisses of the West Highlands. The latter rocks are very similar to some of the Hebridean gneisses. *In areas where rocks of these types occur, the compass is quite unreliable*, but we are unable to say how far this effect is likely to extend beyond the area of outcrop. [*The italics are mine.*]

To sum up then: the rocks of Eriskay are of a type which, when examined elsewhere, have proved to be magnetic. But the range of their magnetic properties is not known; neither is it known (according to Doctor Bullerwell) whether their effect extends over the sea.

At this stage in my inquiries my eye was caught by a caution on Admiralty Chart No. 1796, covering 'Barra Head to Skye and the Small Islands', which reads: 'Local Magnetic Anomalies are reported to exist in the Sea of the Hebrides.' This seemed to indicate that in this area, at any rate, the magnetic properties extended over the sea; and for further details I turned again to the West Coast of Scotland Pilot. Here a number of magnetic anomalies are reported, one under the heading 'Central Part of the Sound of Mull', which it is stated, 'increases the normal magnetic variation by amounts up to six degrees'. No mention of any anomaly is made in the section on the Sound of Eriskay; but this does not, of course, prove that it does not exist. The waters off the Outer Hebrides are much more remote than those off the mainland and around Mull, and are used almost solely by fishermen. Very few yachtsmen venture across the Minch, and larger vessels (very wisely) keep to the orthodox tracks. Also, as already mentioned, the Outer Hebrides have not yet been covered by the Geological Survey.

As indicated by the geologists, the strength of the magnetic pull of the rocks would depend very much on the distance; so the question arises as to how far offshore the *Politician* was at this stage of her journey. When she hit the telegraph cable, as we already know, she was about a mile and a half off. When she came up opposite Ben Stack, in the southern end of Eriskay, she may have been slightly less than a mile off. It is unlikely that she could have come much closer without hitting Binch Rock, or Roderick Rock, or running into a shoal. (It was low water at a period of Neap tides.) But some where about this spot she began veering to the west – this must have been so because she passed to the west of Hartamul and the rocks around it; if she had passed to the other side, she could not have reached Calvay. Between Hartamul and the north east corner of Eriskay (Rosinish Point) the water is relatively deep and clear of obstructions, so such a course would have been possible. The only large obstacle, in fact, between here and the point where she ran aground, is a sandbank about one hundred and thirty yards across. If, however, the ship was on a north west course, she could have skirted the south east corner of it. Admittedly the distance between the sandbank and Rosinish Point is only two hundred yards, and even this is punctuated with a number of small rocks, but it must be remembered that the beam of a ship is relatively small, being measured in feet, and there would have been room for her to squeeze through. Possibly, it was one of these rocks which dented the side of the ship before she came to a halt, causing the fan blade to clatter against it – the incident reported by Huntington. The only other route would haye been round to the north of the sandbank, but this would have involved a violent swing just before she struck, which seems most unlikely. The course suggested, to the south of the sandbank, would have involved a gentle swing over a distance of three miles.

Nevertheless a swing of 60 or more degrees is very considerable over a period of eighteen minutes – that is, between 7.28 and 7.45 am, and the question must be put as to whether it can be accounted for solely by the pull of the lode hill. Is it possible that, somewhere opposite Ben Stack, Swain altered course to the west? As we have seen already the normal track up the Minch involves a course of between due north and 005 degrees; and till 7.28 am anyway, the *Politician* was steaming on a bearing of 015 degrees to 020 degrees – some 15 degrees too far to the east. Did Swain bring her head round to the north to follow the usual track, and so, unknown to him, sail right into the magnetic field of the lode hill? This may be the explanation for his statement which Huntington heard: 'It's my fault. . . it's completely my fault.' Did he believe that if he had not altered course the accident would never have occurred? It would surely seem that if he had interpreted Worthington's orders correctly and taken all reasonable precautions, he would have had nothing to worry about. Or is it possible that Worthington – through laziness or his complete trust – left the course to Swain? Again, Swain's remark is understandable. What is not understandable is that he should have deliberately swung the ship on to a north west course; this, considering its course a few minutes earlier, would have been navigational madness. And if he did not, then the magnetic call of the islands would seem to be the only explanation. There would have been an accident in any case; but it was the final swing to Calvay which ensured that the islands would keep part of the ship for ever.

As a sea mystery, the story of the *Politician* is surely unique in the fact that its secrets remain, even though the entire crew survived, and many of the officers and men are still alive today. Had one man survived from the *Marie Celeste* that famous mystery would have been cleared up immediately; the same would apply to La Peronne's ship, and every case one can think of. But here was a modern ship of 8,000 tons with all its gear working, destroyed in a matter of seconds. Till magnetic tests are carried out up in Eriskay, we can never be certain if a lode hill was responsible, or to what extent. But as I said at the beginning, it is my belief that all legends are true in their own way. . . and that this one is no exception.

After completing the first draft of this book, I received a letter from the cook aboard the *Politician*, Mr H I Strickland. He (like Huntington and Cottrell) thinks that drinking had nothing to do with the accident; he even asserts that none of the crew got at the cargo. His knowledge of Worthington is not great, never having served under him on previous voyages, but from his observations at the time of the accident and afterwards, he formed a very high opinion of him. He thought Swain a capable officer. Regarding the causes of the accident he says that the general opinion below decks was that there were two: 'A faulty compass and the magnetic pull from the rock structure of the islands.'

I also received a letter from Mr D MacDonald, the school-master on Eriskay, who said that in his view the lode hill causing the wrecks around the northern shores of the island was *Meall Ie 'Ill Fhaolain*, McLellan's Hill. The location of this feature confused me at first, as it lies to the *east* of the *Politician*'s course on the coast of South Uist; and to have sent the ship on the rocks, therefore, it would have had to repel the compass needle – something I imagined most unlikely. But inquiries among the scientists soon showed that I was mistaken; if a rock could be charged sufficiently to affect a ship's compass, it could invert it (to use their word) as readily as attract it. Dr Bullerwell was even able to produce a specific example. In the report of the fifth British Association meeting, held in Dublin in 1835, there is a paper by Lloyd, Sabine, and Ross on the subject of magnetic measurements in Ireland. In it they state that:

> A remarkable case . . . has been noted at Fair Head, on the north coast of Ireland. The magnetic polarity of one of the columns which compose this wonderful facade is said to be so strong as to invert the position of the compass needle. . .

And the extraordinary thing is that the basaltic rocks of Fair Head are known to be of the same age and of similar character to those occurring in various places in the Western Isles. So again, local legend and belief may not be so far from the truth.

If, however, *Meall Ie 'Ill Fhaolain* was not directly concerned, it may be that there is so much magnetite in the rocks to the north and south of Calvay that (in Lawrie's phrase) 'the compass is quite unreliable'. Certainly, if one draws a circle, one and a half miles in diameter, cutting through Rosinish Point, Calvay, *Meall Ie 'Ill Fhaolain*, Hartamul, and the Red Rocks, one encloses the whole area in which the wrecks have occurred. What their total number is, it is impossible to say, but apart from the *Ayrshire*, the *Birchol*, and the *Thala*, which have been mentioned already, MacDonald gives the position of three others. If the *Politician* was not in *good* company, she was certainly not the first ship nor the last to be caught up in this mysterious pattern of islands.

CHAPTER 9

The Final Count

LONG AFTER THE LAST prisoner had finished his sentence and McColl and McKenzie had abandoned the search, the islanders still guarded their dwindling stocks of whisky. They became secretive, not mentioning them even to friends and relations, for fear of betrayal. The party spirit had long been dissipated and the hangover of bitterness and mistrust lingered on, not only for months but for years. Even now, in the sixties, feuds born in the days of the *Politician* still exist.

During the post-war years, hundreds of '*Polly* bottles' kept appearing on the machar, their recent owners having taken them some distance from their crofts before disposing of them. Many of the bottles were large, rather handsome Haig 'dimples', and people began bringing them into Miss Shand, at the Highland Industries, asking her if she could make any use of them. At first she declined them, but then had a sudden brainwave, filling them with the white sand from Prince Charlie's Strand (on Eriskay), and turning them into the bases for table lamps. They looked very attractive indeed – I can vouch for this, having seen one belonging to Mrs Mitchell – and sold like hot cakes at the Highland Industries shop in Edinburgh, at fifteen shillings a time – especially to Americans who had seen the film of *Whisky Galore*.

Mention of this film leads inevitably to Sir Compton Mackenzie. Visiting him in Edinburgh, soon after my visit to the islands, I asked if his novel was still selling. He replied that it was, all over the world, and a new edition was being brought out. He added: 'Its fascination must be that it is really a modern fairy story – someone looking for treasure, and finding it.' To me, its great charm is that it does what so few novels do in English literature, that is reflect the life of a whole community, ignoring completely any artificial barriers of class or money. It also has the earthy, healthy tang of a folk novel. Many people, I believe, consider it contains the only successful attempt to capture the flavour of the Gaelic speech of the islanders, and translate it into English. For this novel alone, not to mention the film, I myself shall always be grateful to the *Politician*, and of course to Sir Compton who was, most remarkably, living in the right place at the right time. Just before I left him, he asked me the Captain's name. When I told him it was Beaconsfield Worthington, he smiled. 'What a wonderful name!' he said, wishing perhaps that he had known of it before he wrote the novel.

Towards the end of March, 1941, Huntington met Swain in Liverpool. Swain was no longer worried, and said: 'The inquiry came off all right. I was held not to blame.' A year later, he became master of the *Custodian*, in the Harrison line, and served on till the normal retiring age. Worthington was apparently exonerated as well, as he continued his career at sea, going as master to a captured French ship, the *Arica*. She was later torpedoed off Tobago, Trinidad, with the loss of twenty lives, but Worthington's luck held, and he died in his bed at the age of 84.

Huntington went to the *Philosopher*, then to the *Diplomat*, leaving her the voyage before she was torpedoed. He then went as Second Engineer to Mossman again, this time aboard the *Barrister*. In 1942 they sailed to the Mediterranean, but on returning in December of that year ran on to the rocks at Dingle Bay, on the south coast of Ireland. As the waters poured into the stricken ship, Mossman turned to Huntington and remarked, 'Well, I don't know, Tom. . . we've done it again!'

McColl served on at Lochboisdale till 1949, when he retired. A year or two after the wreck of the *Politician* he suffered severely from his stomach, but recovered and was able to go on till he was 60. Two years later, in 1951, he died of coronary thrombosis. David Shaw, the Procurator-Fiscal, who knew him well during these last years, told me that his conscience was quite clear as to the way he had discharged his duties towards HM Customs. But he did sometimes wonder if he had not been too severe on the islanders, and this worried him. One can quite appreciate the processes by which this change of attitude came about. No longer burdened with official responsibilities and compelled to view things from that specific angle, he allowed his natural sympathies for the islanders to come to the surface, no doubt quite uncon-sciously. Also, he could appreciate now that they were quite right in their contention that the whisky which was not rescued by them might be wasted or destroyed. The stories of rediscoveries of old caches must have brought a wry smile, for now that he was retired no officer was sent to Lochboisdale to succeed him, and it was unlikely that anyone would come down from Stornoway to investigate matters. The Customs had heard enough about the *Politician* to last them for all time.

As the wind blows across the machar, new discoveries keep being made, the sand changing its contours to reveal odd bottles, or cases, or even several cases at a time. Quite a large cache was discovered in 1961, and just before I arrived some bottles were found at Kilpheder. Someone was moving into a new house, happened to strip the thatch off his old croft next door and there they were. The cry 'Polly bottles!' went up, and as it was the week before Christmas, there was a party going as soon as the corks were whipped out. This sort of thing will probably go on as long as there are people living on the islands.

And then there are the thousand cases left in No. 5 hold, at the bottom of the Sound of Eriskay. As might have been expected, many of them were destroyed by the dynamite, but by no means all. At very low tides the wreck is uncovered, and till a few years ago, anyway, fishermen went across to it to see what they could find. Also skin-divers like to search the wreck, and not long ago one of them (from the RAF on Benbecula) rescued a few bottles with the whisky inside them. Not wishing to incur trouble, he contacted the Customs officer at Stornoway, who opened one bottle and sampled the contents. Later he reported to his superiors that 'it was not lethal, but not potable' – the sea having penetrated the cork and succeeded where the salvors, the shipbreakers, and the dynamite had all failed. The Customs are no longer worried about the bottles that are left; if anyone wants to drink them, they are entirely welcome.

Eric Linklater remarks somewhere that the only positive results of wars are that poor men in dingy pubs should have a wealth of memories. In many ways, this is true of the *Politician*. Some will say that this was the greatest saga of the Hebrides in modern times; some that it was an unmitigated disaster. It all depends on one's point of view, and it is difficult to moralize. But to anyone who insists on a moral, one can only state, I think, that faced with these extraordinary circumstances, the rash became rasher, the drunken more drunken, the avaricious more avaricious, the convivial more convivial, the generous more generous, the treacherous more treacherous, the selfish more selfish, and the commercial more commercial. But the fever passed, and as the circumstances became normal so did the people. All that was left was one song and a host of memories, a wealth of stories.

But is it, as some will argue, a condemnation of the islanders that they allowed themselves to submit to this fever in the first place? Well, I only met one man who professed to have remained quite calm and unaffected. He was old and blind when I met him, and he said to me simply: 'No. . . I was not interested in the *Politician*. . . I don't like whisky.' Now I would not like to argue that an appreciation of whisky is an essential part of living; but to me, this old man, compared to Peter MacInnes or Angus John, seemed cold, desiccated, and with a negative air about him, as if he had never really lived. Perhaps it is that our imperfections, follies, and sporadic excesses form part of the process by which we generate warmth, humanity, and finally wisdom. Many of the islanders undoubtedly broke the law; they may have sinned; but that as a consequence they are damned I refuse to believe. There are black sheep in the Hebrides, but so there are in other communities, never blessed or cursed with a *Politician*.

Finally, how much whisky did the islanders rescue? The exact figure will never be known. Personally, I should have thought they got a good third of the cargo – over seven thousand cases – some of which they lost to the Customs and the police. The men I recorded were only a few out of some hundreds who visited the wreck, and yet their total haul was over five hundred cases. Angus John reckoned he got three hundred; and Norman MacMillan and his mates got one hundred and forty-four cases in one night. When they gave me these figures they may have been exaggerating, but there is no proof; and certainly Norman MacMillan seemed one of the most straightforward and reliable men I have ever met in my life. Another point is the large number of cases seized by McColl on the nights he went out in McIsaac's boat: these could only have been a small proportion of the cases taken on these nights, as he could only deal with one or two boats out of all those on the job. And most nights he was not able to go out to sea at all. There is the further point that while he was on South Uist, the whisky was able to flow ashore on to Eriskay and Barra unchecked. Finally, one can argue that if the Customs and the police recovered between one thousand and one thousand five hundred cases, then the total haul must have been several times this amount, as the revelry went on unchecked from Benbecula to Barra, week after week.

Against this, the Customs naturally tend to minimize the loss, basing their estimate on the figures for the loads taken by the coasters to Glasgow from 12 May onwards. But Holden's figures seem to vary from the Customs figures and there even seems to be a doubt as to the exact size of the cargo – whether, for example, the twenty-two thousand cases reported by Gledhill included the large Haig 'dimples' and other fancy bottles. Also, no one can say for certain how many cases were left in the hold when the dynamite went off; or how many were rescued by the islanders even after that. As already mentioned, the charges were not completely effective, and as at very low tides the wreck was above the water-line, boats could still go out to see what could be found. Whatever figure one takes, the total haul (including the loss to the revenue) must have run into tens of thousands of pounds. The whole cargo, when Commander Kay went aboard, must have been worth (on the home market) about £211,000, and this he thought not worth worrying about. No doubt he had his reasons; but it seems an expensive way to inspire a song. . .

So here's a health to the Captain bold
   Of the good ship *Politician*!
And here's to the rock she struck that night
   A-sailing on her mission!
What's left of her can still be found
Off Calvay Isle in Eriskay Sound;
Of all great ships she is renowned –
   The *Polly*!
   The *Polly*!
      We shall not see her like again
      Though we live from now to a hundred and ten,
   The good ship *Politician*!

Index

The Whisky Muse

Robin Laing
ISBN 1 84282 041 9 PBK £7.99

This is a collection of the best poems and songs, both old and new, on the subject of that great Scottish love, whisky. Brought together by Robin Laing, a highly resp-ected Scottish folk-singer and song-writer, and based on his one-man show *The Angel's Share*, it combines two of his passions – folk song and whisky. Each poem and song is accompanied by fascinating addition-al information, and the book is full of interesting tit-bits on the process of whisky making. Lubricated by warmth and companionship – as well as a dram – the Whisky Muse is the spark of inspiration that came to Scotland's great poets and songwriters. Slàinte!

Whisky has been a source of inspira-tion for many centuries. This beauti-fully illustrated collection of 95 poems and songs demonstrates the quality and volume of Scotland's musings upon whisky and its consequences.

Ranging from pre-18th century to contemporary times, and with works by Burns, RLS, MacDiarmid, McGon-agall and many more, a complex identity is revealed in a multiplicity of verse.

Some songs document significant moments, including one written by Robin at the request of Islay's Bruichladdich distillery to commem-orate their re-opening.

Snow's importance to Eskimos is shown in the many different names they give it. Scots do the same with inebriation and their descriptions of whisky recall the taste of 'misty glens, rolling rivers, windswept islands, and toffee-dark peat'.

A well-established musician, Robin Laing takes some of the inspiration that makes Scottish music and whisky noticed, and draws upon experience gained from four CDs and several international tours, to distil whisky's significance – both in Scotland and beyond – into one concentrated vol-ume of verse (including comprehen-sive musical scores).

'This splendid book is necessary reading for anyone interested in whisky and song. It encapsulates Scottish folk culture and the very spirit of Scotland.'
WHISKY MAGAZINE

'One of Scotland's premier folk singer-songwriters.' SUNDAY POST

Rum: Nature's Island

Magnus Magnusson

ISBN 0 946487 32 4 PBK £7.95

Where is the earliest human settlement site yet to be discovered n Scotland?

Which British Prime Minister inherited the island of Rum in 1866?

Why was Rum known as 'the Forbidden Isle' prior to 1957?

To which Scottish castle was John Betjeman referring when he wrote in 1959: 'in time to come the castle will be a place of pilgrimage for all those who want to see how people lived in good King Edward's days'?

Magnus Magnusson answers all these and many other questions in this fascinating story of the Hebridean island of Rum. It moves from earliest times through to the Clearance and its period as the sporting playground of a Lancashire industrial magnate, and on to its rebirth as a National Nature Reserve, a model for the active ecological management of Scotland's wild places.

Thoroughly researched and written in a lively and accessible style, this book includes comprehensive coverage of the island's geology, wildlife, plants, and people, with a special chapter on the Edwardian extravaganza of Kinloch Castle. This 'temple to private indulgence', as Magnusson describes it, cost some £15m in today's terms to create.

There is practical information for the visitors including details of bothy and other accommodation, walks and heritage trails. The book closes with a positive vision for the island's future: biologically diverse, economically dynamic and ecologically sustainable.

Lewis and Harris: History and Pre-history

Francis Thompson

ISBN 0 946487 77 4 PBK £5.99

The fierce Norsemen, intrepid missionaries and mighty Scottish clans – all have left a visible mark on the landscape of Lewis and Harris. This guide explores sites of interest, from pre-history through to the present day.

Harsh conditions failed to deter invaders from besieging these islands or intrepid travellers from settling, and their legacy has stood the test of time in an array of captivating archaeological remains, from the stunningly preserved Carloway Broch to a number of haunting standing stones, tombs and cairns. Telling captivating tales of the places he visits – including an intriguing murder mystery and a romantic encounter resulting in dramatic repercussions for warring clans – Francis Thompson introduces us to his homeland and gives an insight into its forgotten way of life.

Skye 360: Walking the coastline of Skye

Andrew Dempster

ISBN 0 946487 85 5 PBK £8.99

One long walk divided into lots of short walks taking you all the way round Skye's rugged coastline.

Skye's plethora of peninsulas and sea-lochs contain awesome cliffs, remote beaches, storm tossed sea-stacks, natural arches, ancient duns, romantic castles, poignant Clearance settlements, tidal islands and idyllic secluded corners.

If you want to experience Skye in all its fascinating wealth of popular tourist haunts and hidden treasures, then let this book take you on a continuous 360-mile coastal walk around this mythical black island. You will soon find that there is a lot more to discover than the celebrated Cuillin ridge, mecca for walkers and climbers from all over the world.

Andrew Dempster took one month to walk the whole coastline, he describes not just a geographical journey along the intricacies of Skye's coastline but also a historical journey from prehistoric fortified duns to legendary castles, from the distressing remains of black-houses to the stark geometry of the Skye bridge.

Whether you want to follow the author on his month-long trek around the coast, or whether you have a week, a weekend or just want to spend a day exploring a smaller part of the island, *Skye 360* is the perfect guidebook.

The Last Lighthouse

Sharma Krauskopf

ISBN 0 946487 96 0 PBK £7.99

After eight years of sacrifice, working extra hours, visiting lighthouses all over Scotland, and many failed bids, the Krauskopfs' search for a lighthouse home had come to a dead end. Desperate, they went to the Shetland Islands to look at one last lighthouse, Eshaness.

Eshaness Lighthouse stands guard over one of the most beautiful seascapes in the world, with, to the north, the awesome cliffs and stacks of the Grind of the Navir (the Gateways of the Giants), and St Magnus Bay to the south. Built atop a precipitous cliff edge, the station was the last lighthouse designed by a member of the famous Stevenson family of lighthouse engineers. Eshaness is also almost the last lighthouse before you reach the North Pole! Situated on a latitude similar to that of Greenland, it is the last major light before Muckle Flugga, the most northerly in the British Isles.

This Last Lighthouse was a dream come true.

'This book will be a huge inspiration to the thousands of people who dream of living in a lighthouse and/or a remote place. Sharma Krauskopf and her husband Dean spent eight years turning that dream into a reality. Their story ... is one of dogged determination and, ultimately, joy. The at-the-time reporting of their efforts brings immediacy to their quest for a universal dream.' Tim Harrison, EDITOR, LIGHTHOUSE DIGEST, and PRESIDENT, AMERICAN LIGHTHOUSE FOUNDATION

The Road Dance

John MacKay

ISBN 1 84282 040 0 PBK £6.99

Life in the Scottish Hebrides can be harsh – 'The Edge of the World', some call it. For the beautiful Kirsty MacLeod, the love of Murdo and their dreams of America promise an escape from the scrape of the land and the repression of the church. But the Great War looms and Murdo is conscripted. The villages hold a grand Road Dance to send their young men off to battle. As the dancers swirl and sup the wheels of tragedy are set in motion.

Kirsty is overpowered and raped by an unknown assailant. She hides her dark secret, fearful of what it will mean for her and the baby she is carrying. Only the embittered doctor, a man with a cold wife and a colder bed, suspects.

On a fateful day of surging seas and swelling pain Kirsty learns that her love will never be back. Now she must make her choice and it is no choice at all.

'Powerful, shocking, heartbreaking'
DAILY MAIL

'With a gripping plot that subtly twists and turns, vivid characterisation and a real sense of time and tradition, this is an absorbing, powerful first novel. The impression it made on me will remain for some time.'
THE SCOTS MAGAZINE

Heartland

John MacKay

ISBN 1 905222 11 4 PBK £6.99

This was his land. He had sprung from it and would surely return to it. Its pure air refreshed him, the big skies inspired him and the pounding seas were the rhythm of his heart. It was his touchstone. Here he renourished his soul.

A man tries to build for his future by reconnecting with his past, leaving behind the ruins of the life he has lived. Iain Martin hopes that by returning to his Hebridean roots and embarking on a quest to reconstruct the ancient family home, he might find new purpose.

But as Iain begins working on the old blackhouse, he uncovers a secret from the past, which forces him to question everything he ever thought to be true.

Who can he turn to without betraying those to whom he is closest? His ailing mother, his childhood friend and his former love are both the building – and stumbling – blocks to his new life.

Where do you seek sanctuary when home has changed and will never be the same again?

'Heartland will hopefully keep readers turning the pages. It is built on an exploration of the ties to people and place, and of knowing who you are.'
JOHN MACKAY

'. . . Atmospheric little gem.'
THE HERALD

THE QUEST FOR

The Quest for the Celtic Key
Karen Ralls-MacLeod and Ian Robertson
ISBN 1 84282 084 2 PBK £7.99

The Quest for the Nine Maidens
Stuart McHardy
ISBN 0 946487 66 9 HBK £16.99

The Quest for Charles Rennie Mackintosh
John Cairney
ISBN 1 84282 058 3 HBK £16.99

The Quest for Robert Louis Stevenson
John Cairney
ISBN 0 946487 87 1 HBK £16.99

The Quest for the Original Horse Whisperers
Russell Lyon
ISBN 1 84282 020 6 HBK £16.99

ON THE TRAIL OF

On the Trail of the Pilgrim Fathers
J. Keith Cheetham
ISBN 0 946487 83 9 PBK £7.99

On the Trail of Mary Queen of Scots
J. Keith Cheetham
ISBN 0 946487 50 2 PBK £7.99

On the Trail of John Wesley
J. Keith Cheetham
ISBN 1 84282 023 0 PBK £7.99

On the Trail of William Wallace
David R. Ross
ISBN 0 946487 47 2 PBK £7.99

On the Trail of Robert the Bruce
David R. Ross
ISBN 0 946487 52 9 PBK £7.99

On the Trail of Robert Service
GW Lockhart
ISBN 0 946487 24 3 PBK £7.99

On the Trail of John Muir
Cherry Good
ISBN 0 946487 62 6 PBK £7.99

On the Trail of Robert Burns
John Cairney
ISBN 0 946487 51 0 PBK £7.99

On the Trail of Bonnie Prince Charlie
David R Ross
ISBN 0 946487 68 5 PBK £7.99

On the Trail of Queen Victoria in the Highlands
Ian R Mitchell
ISBN 0 946487 79 0 PBK £7.99

On the Trail of Scotland's Myths and Legends
Stuart McHardy
ISBN 1 84282 049 4 PBK £7.99

LUATH GUIDES TO SCOTLAND

The North West Highlands: Roads to the Isles
Tom Atkinson
ISBN 1 84282 086 9 PBK £5.99

Mull and Iona: Highways and Byways
Peter Macnab
ISBN 1 84282 089 3 PBK £5.99

The Northern Highlands: The Empty Lands
Tom Atkinson
ISBN 1 84282 087 7 PBK £5.99

The West Highlands: The Lonely Lands
Tom Atkinson
ISBN 1 84282 088 5 PBK £5.99

NATURAL WORLD

The Hydro Boys: pioneers of renewable energy
Emma Wood
ISBN 1 84282 047 8 PBK £8.99

Wild Lives: Otters – On the Swirl of the Tide
Bridget MacCaskill
ISBN 0 946487 67 7 PBK £9.99

Wild Lives: Foxes – The Blood is Wild
Bridget MacCaskill
ISBN 0 946487 71 5 PBK £9.99

Scotland – Land & People: An Inhabited Solitude
James McCarthy
ISBN 0 946487 57 X PBK £7.99

The Highland Geology Trail
John L Roberts
ISBN 0 946487 36 7 PBK £5.99

Luath Press Limited

committed to publishing well written books worth reading

LUATH PRESS takes its name from Robert Burns, whose little collie Luath (*Gael.*, swift or nimble) tripped up Jean Armour at a wedding and gave him the chance to speak to the woman who was to be his wife and the abiding love of his life. Burns called one of *The Twa Dogs* Luath after Cuchullin's hunting dog in *Ossian's Fingal*. Luath Press was established in 1981 in the heart of Burns country, and is now based a few steps up the road from Burns' first lodgings on Edinburgh's Royal Mile. Luath offers you distinctive writing with a hint of unexpected pleasures.

Most bookshops in the UK, the US, Canada, Australia, New Zealand and parts of Europe either carry our books in stock or can order them for you. To order direct from us, please send a £sterling cheque, postal order, international money order or your credit card details (number, address of cardholder and expiry date) to us at the address below. Please add post and packing as follows: UK – £1.00 per delivery address; overseas surface mail – £2.50 per delivery address; overseas airmail – £3.50 for the first book to each delivery address, plus £1.00 for each additional book by airmail to the same address. If your order is a gift, we will happily enclose your card or message at no extra charge.

Luath Press Limited
543/2 Castlehill
The Royal Mile
Edinburgh EH1 2ND
Scotland
Telephone: 0131 225 4326 (24 hours)
Fax: 0131 225 4324
email: gavin.macdougall@luath.co.uk
Website: www.luath.co.uk